REASONS II

REASONS

II

Sects and Cults with Christian Roots

Bill Evenhouse

Bible Way

Grand Rapids, Michigan

Library of Congress Cataloging in Publication Data

Evenhouse, Bill, 1939–
   Reasons II, sects and cults with Christian roots.

   Bibliography: p.
   1. Christian sects.   2. Cults.   3. Apologetics—20th century.
I. Title.   II. Title: Sects and cults with Christian roots.
BR157.E73   289   81-10229
ISBN 0-933140-25-8   AACR2

First printing, 1981
Second printing, 1984

Always be prepared to give an answer to everyone who asks you to give the reason for the hope that you have. But do this with gentleness and respect. . . .
1 Peter 3:15–16 (NIV)

Contents

Preface

This is the second in a series of four books in the course entitled Reasons. *That title is borrowed from Peter's injunction to "Always be prepared. . .to give the reason for the hope that you have." It's a course that's intended to help Reformed Christians give reasons for their faith when conversing with people who hold another faith.*

Reasons *is offered as part of the BIBLE WAY curriculum for young adults. That doesn't mean that this book and course won't be profitable for you if you don't think of yourself as falling in that rather vague category.* Reasons *is usable by a variety of age groups, from mature high school seniors to the oldest adults. Christians of all ages should learn to give reasons for what they believe.*

Still, sects and cults, other faiths, and different understandings of the Christian faith are a particular concern for young people in their very late teens and early twenties. Those are often unsettled years when young men and women are leaving home communities and finding their own niche in life. The instability that comes with such a basic life change can make otherwise well-adjusted people peculiarly vulnerable to the lure of some offbeat religious groups and strange new ideas.

This book will introduce you to eight sects and cults with Christian roots. It's intended to prepare you, as a Christian, to understand the teachings and attractions of these groups and to speak to their adherents.

The author of this book is Mr. William Evenhouse. A native of Grand Rapids, Michigan, Mr. Evenhouse graduated from Calvin College and the University of Michigan (M.A. in Creative Writing). After teaching in the United States for several years and doing further graduate work in linguistics, he went to Nigeria for the Christian Reformed Board of World Missions and worked there from 1965 to 1980 as a teacher and linguist. He is presently employed in the Curriculum Department of Christian Schools International.

Background research for this book required an expert's in-depth knowledge and perception. These were provided by Dr. J. William Smit, professor of sociology at Calvin College. A graduate of that institution and of the University of Michigan, Dr. Smit has a special interest in the sociology of religion.

The session guides in this book were prepared by the Education Department staff.

Harvey A. Smit
Director of Education

MAKING AN APOLOGY

Reasons is a course in apologetics. That's a field of theological study and not—as the word seems to suggest—a way of saying you're sorry.

The word *apologetics* comes from ancient Athens. When an Athenian citizen was charged with some crime or illegal action, he had the right to defend himself publicly before his fellow citizens. That defense was called an apology. It was a public defense of his own actions.

The Bible uses this same word several times. In Acts 19, for instance, when the people of Ephesus were upset by Paul's preaching, Alexander, a local believer, stood up and tried to make a defense or apology for Paul (v. 33). Also, the apostle Peter warns Christians spread throughout Asia Minor and facing imminent persecution: "Always be prepared to make a defense [apology] to anyone who calls you to account for the hope that is in you..." (1 Pet. 3:15 RSV).

Apologetics then is the study of how Christians may best defend their faith. *Reasons* is a course designed to help you make such apologies.

According to Peter's clear injunction, defending the faith is something each of us should be prepared to do. Christian philosophers often make such a defense in writing against non-Christian or anti-Christian thinkers. In the same way ordinary believers should be prepared to defend the faith while conversing with non-Christian people across the backyard fence or at the office party.

Doing apology clearly does *not* mean apologizing for Christ or making excuses for what you believe or how you act. Instead it means you should be ready to say what you believe and explain why you believe as you do whenever you are challenged to do so. If a convinced Baptist asks why you were baptized as an infant, if friends inquire why you won't join them for a Sunday morning golf game, if Jehovah's Witnesses come to your door and want to know why you won't visit their Kingdom Hall, or if a co-worker asks why you refuse to take any moral shortcuts—you should be able to give reasons, faith-reasons, why you act as you do. That kind of defense is one of the obligations of the Christian faith.

Making such apologies is important partly for your own sake (How can anyone be confident in a faith that can't be defended or reasonably explained?) and partly for the sake of others (How else can anyone see the attraction of the gospel except as it immediately relates to a believer's life?). So for both yourself and for your neighbor's good, being prepared to give reasons for your faith is a valuable exercise.

This textbook, *Reasons II,* is intended to help prepare you to make apology to members of various sects and cults with Christian roots. What do we mean by sects and cults?

Generally a religious group is called a cult if it makes a definite break with the traditional religion of the society. Cults usually claim some special revelation from God by which they reinterpret or add to the generally accepted religious writings (Bible, Koran, etc.). Cults also are usually built around a strong leader who insists on strict discipline and has absolute authority over his or her followers. Cults, if they last long enough, may become a new religion. Jehovah's Witnesses are an example of a cult.

A sect, on the other hand, is a small religious group that has broken with some traditional religious system or denomination but has not done so radically. A sect is usually trying to get back to the original true faith, not found a radically new faith. It still accepts the religious writings of the main group as authoritative. Sects tend more toward lay leadership and permit more individualism than cults do. The Hutterites are an example of a Christian sect.

The line between sects and cults isn't absolute, but it's still important. Because of the different quality of leadership and kind of authority recognized, one generally deals differently with disciples of a cult than with members of a sect.

This book contains eight challenges, each of which treats a specific sect or cult. These challenges try to give you not only some basic information about this religious group but also the flavor of these people's faith—why they believe and act as they do and why they are able to attract others into their group. The challenge is finally intended, as the name implies, to invite you to respond, to summon you to consider what you would say or do if you happened to meet such a person.

We're asking you, together with others who are taking this course, to consider that challenge and how you might best respond. A group discussion should help you recognize the strengths and weaknesses of your own church's position, how prepared or unprepared you are to make such an apology, and what the best approach might be. A session guide follows each challenge. It is designed to offer some direction to your class discussion.

After the group discussion (or sometime during it), we've suggested that your teacher or discussion leader hand out the author's response to the challenge. The approach the author takes is not the one authoritative answer, the only good way to respond. You may disagree with it. You may have already reached some other conclusion. Still each response will give you, for future reference, the thoughtful ideas of someone who has studied this group with care. An envelope has been provided on the back cover of this book for storing the author's responses.

It's our earnest hope that this course will not only strengthen your understanding of your own faith, but also begin to equip you to deal confidently and positively with believers of various sects and cults. It's with that hope that we offer this book for your study.

Harvey A. Smit
Director of Education

Mass Baptisms of Jehovah's Witnesses,
Shea Stadium, New York, 1978

JEHOVAH'S WITNESSES

Founding: Charles Taze Russell of Alleghany City, Pennsylvania (USA), founded this special group of Second Adventists in the early 1870s. Called variously the Millennial Dawn, the International Bible Students Association, and the Watchtower Association, the popular present name was given by the Witnesses' second president, J. F. Rutherford. He based the name Jehovah's Witnesses on the prophet Isaiah's words, "Ye are my witnesses, saith Jehovah" (43:10).

Following: The Witnesses claim some two million active members (called publishers). Of these 175,000 live in Canada, 530,000 in the United States. There are perhaps another two million occasional or associated members. The Witnesses are present in some 210 countries and their literature is published in 78 languages.

Faith: The Witnesses believe in an Almighty God, a single person not a Trinity, who is called Jehovah, the Creator of the heavens and the earth. They also believe:

　　*The Bible is God's Word and all their teachings are taken from the Bible.

　　*Christ is not God. He is the archangel Michael, who is God's first creation. Christ is God's Son, but he is still inferior to God. He died on a stake as a ransom paid for obedient believers. He was resurrected as an immortal spirit creature.

　　*The most obedient people will form the little flock of 144,000 who will go to heaven and rule with Christ. Other sheep, by following Christ's example, can earn eternal life.

*The human soul ceases to exist at death and resurrection is the only hope for future life.

*Transfusions of blood or drinking blood are against God's law.

*Baptism must be by complete immersion.

*The Sabbath applied only to the Jews.

*There should be no clergy.

*Every Christian must give public testimony of his or her faith.

I could tell they were Jehovah's Witnesses, partly because salesmen around here usually come alone and partly because it was Saturday, the day when a bunch of them usually fan out from the Kingdom Hall a few blocks down the street.

My mother used to instruct me not to let them in. "They are enemies of our Lord," she would say, "and I want nothing to do with them." She used to say lots more things like that, but lately, maybe considering me old enough to think for myself, she's tapered off a bit. Anyway, she was out shopping (which always means she won't be home till after lunch), and I was bored with the kids programs on TV, so I invited them into our living room.

"Are you really enemies of the Lord?" I began, trying to get the jump on them. It sounded a bit blunt after I said it, so I added, "That's what my mother says."

The woman, who later introduced herself as Maria, winced. "All your people say that," she said. I guessed she meant all the people of my church—in our neighborhood we outnumber the rest about two to one. "And it really makes me feel bad because we preach the good news of salvation through Jesus Christ as faithfully as we can. Do you know 1 Peter 2:24?"

I hesitated, thinking maybe they had a trick up their sleeves. But finally I decided I'd better be honest. "Not offhand," I admitted.

" 'He himself bore our sins in his own body. . . . And by his stripes you were healed.' What about John 3:16?"

"That I know," I said and quoted it.

"That only-begotten Son is the Jesus we believe in," Sam, Maria's fiancé, explained.

"Wait a minute," I said, trying to remember a few more things Mother had said. "How can you say God loved the world so much and then claim that only 144,000 people will be saved?"

Sam and Maria smiled at each other. "Who says that?" Maria asked.

"You Jehovah's Witnesses. Out of all the earth's billions of people, only 144,000 saved!"

Sam answered calmly. "Usually I'd begin by dis-

It was at his baptism that Jesus was "born again."

The Watchtower, November 15, 1954, p. 681

The very fact that he was sent proves he was not equal with God but less than God the Father.

"The Word" Who is He? p. 41
(from Salem Kirban, Jehovah's Witnesses, Doctrines of Devils, No. 3, p. 54)

cussing other issues with you—because we're here to witness, not to argue. But I want to answer your question about God's love and the 144,000 directly. First, though, could you tell me how many people are saved?"

"No," I said, "except it's all those people who have faith in Jesus Christ."

"What about those who don't have that faith?"

"They are lost," I said.

"Where are they?" Maria asked. I thought of telling her I didn't know where they were because they were lost, but that was just a joke I'd read somewhere—and besides she looked very serious.

"They'll all go to hell," I said.

"For how long?"

"For all eternity," I said slowly.

Sam folded his hands and looked first at Maria, then at me. "To answer your question about the 144,000— Revelation 14:1–3 says very plainly that 144,000 people who have been brought from the earth are with the Lamb standing upon Mount Zion. But we do not teach that the 'little flock' are the only ones who receive salvation. Many, many more will inhabit the new earth. Jesus calls them his other sheep in John 10:16. Revelation 7:9 says they are a great crowd beyond number.

"We recognize Jehovah is a God of love. He saves a great number—some to reign in heaven and some to live in perfect comfort and joy on earth. You, on the other hand, talk of an eternal punishment for some in hell. How can you speak of a God of love who chooses to save some humans but punishes others eternally? You see, the problem is *yours,* not ours."

"You don't believe in hell?" I asked. This was something Mom hadn't mentioned. "Isn't there a verse that says something about a place where the lost burn in fire?"

"Do you know where the verse is?" Maria asked.

I was beginning to think I should have paid more attention in church school. But I stayed honest. "No, I'm not sure."

But she knew. "One place is Matthew 5:22. The phrase hell fire was translated from *Gehenna,* the word for the garbage dump outside of Jerusalem where fires were always burning. What it means here is that a person could be completely destroyed because of his evil. These verses talk about complete destruction, not about eternal punishment. What would be more cruel: to destroy something or punish it forever?"

"To punish it forever, I guess," I said, feeling a bit nervous. I knew what was coming next.

"Then you believe God is more cruel than we do. But of course that's because you have problems understanding the soul. You think or rather believe it's immortal."

"Isn't it?" I said.

Sam took over. "Let's examine the Scriptures; they should be our teachers. Ezekiel 18:4 says, 'The soul that is sinning, it shall die.' And in Acts, Peter quotes Moses when he says, 'any soul that does not listen to that Prophet will be destroyed.' How could Peter and Moses and Ezekiel all talk about the soul being destroyed if it really could not be destroyed?"

By this time I was really uncomfortable, but Maria and Sam seemed completely at ease. I offered them some Sprite and a couple of Mom's oatmeal cookies. I was hoping I could get my thoughts together by the time they finished the snack. Unfortunately I wasn't in much better shape when they asked the next question.

"Would you say that in general you are satisfied with the condition of the world we live in?"

Now how could anyone trick me on that question? Every newspaper was telling every reader that the crime rate in our city had doubled in the last year. Russia was ready to pounce on its nearest neighbors, and unemployment was the reason I was staying home on nice summer mornings like this one.

"I'd say the world is in a mess," I said. "But I really don't see what I as an individual can do about it."

Maria this time. "Probably the first thing to know is that the Bible speaks directly about our own times."

"It does?" I said, trying not to laugh. "I thought it was all written down by about the year 300."

That didn't faze them. They showed me an excerpt from an 1876 article in which one of their earliest leaders predicted 1914 as the year in which human his-

The doctrine of a burning hell where the wicked are tortured eternally after death cannot be true, mainly for four reasons: (1) it is wholly unscriptural; (2) it is unreasonable; (3) it is contrary to God's love; and (4) it is repugnant to justice.

Let God Be True, p. 99
(from Salem Kirban, *Jehovah's Witnesses, Doctrines of Devils, No. 3*, p. 74)

tory would face a turning point. They knew all sorts of Bible verses which proved that was a correct prediction.

I was beginning to understand my mother's approach. By now I was as washed out as a dishrag, and they were still going strong. Sam and Maria could back up everything they said with a piece of Scripture. And *I* couldn't wiggle out of the position they were putting me in. Don't get me wrong; they were really sweet people. It's just that they were nailing me to the wall. I agreed there should only be one true church. I agreed that the church had to respect God's Word. I agreed that it should sanctify God's name. I agreed that the Bible told us to separate from the world. Finally I agreed that I ought to at least visit a Kingdom Hall or subscribe to their publication—if only to find out more about the truth.

Luckily I didn't have to set a time to visit or to confess I was out of small change to buy anything. Just when I was about to promise to show up at 9:30 A.M. the next day—which would have meant making up something crazy to tell Mom so she'd let me skip church—I noticed Mom's car coming up the drive. For once in her life she'd decided to skip lunch at the shopping mall.

"I hate to bring this to a close," I said, "but my mom'll have a fit. She has this thing about you guys. So though I wish we could continue, I've got to get you out of here."

They understood and were a bit amused I thought. I got them out the front door just as Mom came in the back.

"Who were your friends, Charlie?" she asked. Mom always checked.

"Just kids from down the block. We tried your cookies."

"Not Jehovah's Witnesses?"

"Mom," I said, gently as I could. "You know me. I wouldn't have let them in your living room, would I?"

"I'm not sure," she said. "At any rate your friends forgot some of their books. Or maybe they meant to trade them for the cookies." She held up a bright yellow pamphlet.

Some days I'm born to lose.

FOR FURTHER READING

Hoekema, Anthony. *The Four Major Cults.* Grand Rapids, Mich.: Wm. B. Eerdmans Pub. Co., 1963.

Offers a thorough, scholarly look at the Witness cult, particularly at their teachings (pp. 223–371). Looks in detail at how the Witnesses distort Scripture. All chapters of *The Four Major Cults* are also available as separate paperback books (Eerdmans, 1973).

"Jehovah's Witnesses in the Twentieth Century." New York: Watchtower Bible and Tract Society, 1979.

An introduction (31 pages) to the Witnesses from their point of view. Offers a chart of their beliefs, with Scripture references. Probably can be obtained from your local Kingdom Hall.

Kirban, Salem. *Jehovah's Witnesses, Doctrines of Devils, No. 3.* Chicago: Moody Press, 1973.

A short (77 pages) illustrated book. Has a major section contrasting Witness teachings with those of the Bible.

Rosten, Leo. *Religions of America.* New York: Simon and Schuster, 1975.

In twelve pages Milton G. Henschel, director of the Watch Tower Bible and Tract Society of Pennsylvania, offers a number of questions and answers about the Witnesses.

Schnell, William. *Thirty Years a Watchtower Slave.* Grand Rapids, Mich.: Baker Book House, 1971.

An account of a former Witness. Gives "insider" insights into the cult.

Stan, Thomas. *Jehovah's Witnesses and What They Believe.* Grand Rapids, Mich.: Zondervan, 1967.

Another insider's look at the Watchtower cult. Offers advice on how to approach Witnesses.

The Watchtower. New York: Watchtower Bible and Tract Society.

This Witness magazine is required reading for all members. Contains discussions of religious topics, letters from Witnesses, offical replies to questions, suggestions for almost all aspects of living. Printed in over forty languages. Probably available at your local Kingdom Hall.

CASSETTE TAPES

Martin, Walter. *Jehovah's Witnesses, Jesus Christ, and the Holy Trinity.* C-37. Available from the Christian Research Institute, Box 500, San Juan Capistrano, California 92693. Write for brochure and price list.

A Kingdom Hall

SESSION GUIDE

CHALLENGE 1   JEHOVAH'S WITNESSES

A. Personal notes/questions on Challenge 1

B. The teachings of this cult

1. Charlie says that the Witnesses are nailing him to the wall. What accounts for Charlie's poor showing?

2. What specific Witness teachings was Charlie unable to biblically refute?

3. Look back to the first page of this challenge and check out the other beliefs of the Witnesses. Take some time to ask and discuss questions you might have.

C. A Bible study: Witness vs. Christian on the divinity of Christ

The Witnesses state in their own literature that although Christ is the Son of God, he is inferior to God (Jehovah). Your teacher will present the case for the Witnesses, using passages they recommend in their literature. Afterwards, the class will be asked to use Scripture to refute the Witness arguments.

Notes

D. Practical suggestions: what to do when Witnesses call

Mary Baker Eddy

CHRISTIAN SCIENCE

Founding: In 1866 Mrs. Mary Baker Eddy of Boston, Massachusetts, was injured in a serious fall on icy pavement. She claims to have healed herself instantly by certain principles revealed to her. She began to teach this system of healing to pupils. In 1875 the initial draft of her book, *Science and Health with Key to the Scriptures,* appeared. Four years later the Mother Church of Christian Science was organized in Boston.

Following: On its 100th anniversary in 1979, the Christian Science denomination appears to have had over two hundred thousand members organized into more than three thousand churches in over fifty countries. The vagueness of these figures is partially due to Mrs. Eddy's opposition to membership statistics. Members are often of an intellectual, philosophical bent and are dominantly female (75–80 percent female in the United States).

Faith: Christian Scientists believe their religion is Christian (based wholly on the teachings of Jesus Christ in Scripture) and scientific (exact in premise and conclusion and completely demonstrable).
    Some of their beliefs appear to be:
    *Matter is not real. Nothing exists except the divine (immortal) Mind. God is a principle, not a person.
    *People are made in God's image and are not material (mortal) but spiritual (immortal). People are incapable of sin, sickness,

and death. These things are illusions which occur because human minds are not completely given over to the spiritual, the immortal.

*Sin is error; it must be conquered (forgiven) by denying its power or presence, just as Christ—the Way-shower—did on the cross. Salvation means deliverance from any awareness of pain or evil.

*Jesus was not divine; he was human. Only the immortal principle in him (Christ) was true deity. Jesus did not arise from the dead or ascend into heaven—Christ did, because he is eternal and spiritual.

*Mrs. Eddy's writings (*Science and Health*) must be used to interpret the Bible.

Dearest Niece,

I could see, Mary—anyone could have seen—that you were angry and frustrated when you left my house yesterday. I watched as you stalked down the flagstone walk, taking no notice of the beautiful flowers I planted yesterday. And I spent the next few minutes imagining the monologue that was running through your mind.

That stubborn old woman, you must have been saying, *she'll probably be dead by tomorrow. If she'd let me take her temperature, she'd have to admit she had a fever. We could rush her to the hospital, give her oxygen and antibiotics, and have her up and around in a day or two. But she fears medicine more than pneumonia.*

Since I'm still alive today and have every intention of returning to my gardening tomorrow, I've decided to make good use of this rest I'm enjoying by composing a "real" answer to your "imaginary" complaints. Actually, I'm far from crazy and a good deal younger than that frantically energetic sister of mine you know as your mother. But more important to me, I *am* your aunt, and I love you as if you were my own daughter. I'd like to "have my cake and eat it too"—to be understood by you and yet avoid arguments, which as always I detest.

How I wish you accepted the teachings of Christian Science. If you did, you would immediately understand what I must say here. But the teachings of your church, mired as they are in a belief in the material world, make it difficult, if not impossible, for you to understand easily what I have to say. If you could "come apart and rest awhile." Or if you would only be willing to read *Science and Health*—but we've gone over that before. So let me just put my thoughts on paper, and you may do with them what you will.

What is it we both want? Health, certainly. You believe I must recover from a sickness caused by microbes or viruses (I admit I'm no authority on today's medicine) to enjoy a few more years with my flowers and my friends. And I want to recover as fervently as you want me to, but from a much more comprehensive disease than you may have diagnosed.

The emphatic purpose of Christian Science is the healing of sin; and this task, sometimes, may be harder than the cure of disease; because, while mortals love to sin, they do not love to be sick.

Mary Baker Eddy.
Thomas Linton Leishman, *Why I Am a Christian Scientist,* p. 23

. . . Christ's command: "Be ye therefore perfect," [means] "Be ye perfect now, this very moment."

Clara Clemens, *Awake to a Perfect Day, My Experience with Christian Science,* p. 39

31

The disease I speak of is the belief that matter or material existence is real and important—that God, who is all goodness and all power and love and truth itself, would allow or permit error or sickness to occur. Such a belief is a disease indeed; it was the source of my greatest despair before I became a Christian Scientist.

Does this make you think I cannot feel the burning of the fever or the searing of my lungs when I gasp for breath? Not at all, but that I endure these things is less important than that I recognize them for what they are: the illusions that would destroy, if I let them, my confidence that I am a perfect child of a perfect God. Would God, the all-in-all, create a universe in which any of his children suffered? Approach God from the viewpoint of divine Mind, and the question answers itself.

You will think I am presenting you with an argument. But I desire no arguments. Mrs. Eddy writes, "If one would not quarrel with his fellow man for waking him from a cataleptic nightmare, he should not resist Truth, which banishes—yea forever destroys with the higher testimony of Spirit—the so-called evidence of matter" (*Science and Health,* p. 128).

What truth does is demonstrate, not argue. Jesus said, "Ye shall know the truth and the truth shall make you free." A set of doctrines which *do* nothing for you is worse than useless. Truth *frees* one from illusion.

You thought I was sick yesterday, and by your definition I was. But today, as I am more deeply aware of my participation, my existence in eternal Mind, the so-called sickness you saw is almost completely eradicated. Tomorrow I may decide to visit *you.* No medicines from either the drugstore or the doctors could have done that. But I knew healing was taking place even before you left. I had placed a call to a practitioner for whom I have the highest regard. He gave me the counsel I needed and undertook prayer to strengthen my faith.

One proof may not be sufficient for you—though faith healings ought to shake the very foundations of so-called medical science. But the proofs are numerous. When I was newly married, only eighteen, and just beginning to understand Christian Science, I attended a football game with your Uncle Bob. One of the struts of the bleacher we were sitting on collapsed, and thirty or forty people were thrown violently to the ground. Several persons were badly injured; two died in a hospital the next day. With his usual agility, your uncle avoided all injury; but I was unable to move, my left leg severely scraped and bleeding, and my back cruelly wrenched.

I met with the most violent objections when I refused hospitalization, but I knew this accident was given to me as an opportunity to experience whether the divine Mind was indeed a reality. At home, in my own bedroom, I put aside every thought of the friends surrounding me and fixed my mind on this prayer: "God in whom I have real being, I know this pain is not part of you. Let me rest in the Christ who healed the sick and raised Lazarus." My friends soon realized I had fallen into a peaceful sleep. When I awoke the next day, they were gone—except my husband, of course—and the pain was gone too. I had the deepest awareness that my "injuries" were the product of mortal mind, which is ever deceitful, and that in reality I remained sound and well. I got out of bed to discover that the injuries had left no effect whatsoever. Even the abrasions on my left leg had disappeared without a trace.

Mrs. Eddy has written: "The same power which heals sin heals also sickness. This is the beauty of holiness, 'that when Truth heals the sick, it casts out evils, and when Truth casts out the evil called disease, it heals the sick.' " I have proved this over and over with my mortal body, and thus I stand in a different relation to these words than you who would insist on fighting "the evil called disease" with medicines. We could truly be said to be "worlds apart."

You argue, when I permit it, that your primary concern is my denial of Jesus Christ. But Paul says, "Let this mind be in you which was also in Christ Jesus." Certainly the "mind" which was in Christ Jesus did not heal through the medicines of that day.

Jesus, as a man, was fully human. In that respect he differed little from you and me—"like unto us, sin ex-

Matter says, "I am the kind of stuff that is real. I have medical laws and physical laws, and you just can't do anything about me because I am substance. Because I am real, spiritual healings cannot happen." This silent argument can be extremely vigorous and obstinate. But all you need is one instance of Mind-healing to undo the argument and to prove that matter is not what it says it is. And that becomes the turning point from matter to Mind.

Homer E. Newell, "Man and the Universe—Matter or Mind?" *Living Christian Science*, p. 249

For the first time I understood that Jesus was the human man, but Christ was the divine Truth— Christ was the way Jesus thought, lived, and taught! And this Christ, Truth, was the Savior of mankind from all its troubles. To follow Christ meant I was to know this Truth as Jesus did, and to let it guide my life.

Adele Bok, "Search and Discovery in Indonesia," *Living Christian Science*, p. 11

cepted." He was free from sin because he was free from illusions about the world: the truth, the Christ was in him. You will call many of his acts miracles because you fail to see those acts as perfectly conforming to divine Mind. But he promised his disciples they would do the same sorts of things and more. And they did; they even raised the dead!

No, my dear niece, I do not deny Jesus Christ. It is by the power of that Christ that I cast out the evil of disease in my body. And when age and time seem to defeat this mortal body, it is in the Truth, in the Christ, that I shall not see death but pass on into eternal Life, Love, Spirit—Immortal Truth.

I often used to wonder why this realization of the divine reality was not immediately obvious to Christians who *know* that sin, disease, and death are to be conquered through Christ. But I have reached the conclusion that unless they will agree to carefully study Mrs. Eddy's *Science and Health,* they will not be able to understand. So much mortal error has crept into the Christian church since apostolic times that one cannot *do* without Mrs. Eddy's key to unlock the spiritual truths. I urge you to read it.

When you see me next, I shall be totally recovered. You will say it was a miracle, but I know it is only what I expect from God, the all-in-all: true health, freedom from sin and error. If I do my part and recognize the reality of Spirit and the illusion of matter, my health, both physical and mental, will be a matter of course.

Love,
Aunt Betty

FOR FURTHER READING

Note: All Christian Science churches have reading rooms, open to the public, where visitors may borrow or purchase books.

Eddy, Mary Baker. *Science and Health with Key to the Scriptures.* Boston: First Church of Christ, Scientist, 1875.

> Worth looking at to see how Christian Science interprets the Scriptures.

Facts about Christian Science. Boston: Christian Science Publishing Society, USA, 1959.

> A twenty-one-page booklet of basic information in question-and-answer format.

Hoekema, Anthony A. *Christian Science.* Grand Rapids, Mich.: Wm. B. Eerdmans Pub. Co., 1974.

> Offers an in-depth study of Christian Science from a biblical point of view. The same material is printed in one chapter of *The Four Major Cults.*

Rosten, Leo. *Religions of America.* New York: Simon and Schuster, 1975.

> Features a chapter (about 12 pages) of questions and answers about the Christian Science Church as expressed by a member of that church and approved by the Mother Church in Boston. Easy to read.

CASSETTE TAPES

Martin, Walter. *Christian Science Healing: Devilish or Divine?* C-74. A single cassette available from the Christian Research Institute, Box 500, San Juan Capistrano, California 92693. Write for prices and brochure.

First Church of Christ, Scientist and (left) Christian Science Publishing Society, Boston, Massachusetts

SESSION GUIDE

CHALLENGE 2   CHRISTIAN SCIENCE

A. Personal notes/questions on Challenge 2

B. Try this true/false quiz to check your knowledge of Christian Science

_____ 1. In Challenge 2 Aunt Betty says her sickness is an illusion.

_____ 2. Though physically ill by our standards, she feels no pain whatever.

_____ 3. If Aunt Betty gets sick enough, she'll probably voluntarily go to a hospital as most Christian Scientists do when seriously ill.

_____ 4. Aunt Betty argues that Christians are stuck with a God who is supposed to be good, but who allows evil, sin, and disease to occur.

_____ 5. Christian Scientists get around this problem (above) by simply denying that sin and disease exist, except in our minds.

_____ 6. Aunt Betty does not believe in a life after death.

_____ 7. Like all Christian Scientists, Aunt Betty believes Christ is not fully divine.

_____ 8. Christian Scientists say that Christ died to show us by his example how to overcome sin and suffering and death.

_____ 9. Christian Scientists are concerned only with the healing of the body, not with the healing of other "wounds" in our society—such as crime, poverty, and loneliness.

_____ 10. As Christians we reject any kind of miraculous healing except those "miracles" performed by legitimate medicine and doctors.

_____ 11. Not a single documented case clearly shows that someone was healed using Christian Science methods.

_____ 12. Mrs. Eddy, founder of Christian Science, claimed a special revelation from God taught her how to heal herself.

_____ 13. Christian Scientists place Mrs. Eddy's book, *Science and Health,* on a par with Scripture.

_____ 14. Christian Science calls itself a *science* because of its belief that modern scientific discoveries will bring about complete human happiness and even salvation.

_____ 15. Christian Scientists have little to do with other Christians, whom they regard as enemies.

_____ 16. Christian Scientists have an aggressive evangelism program, similar to that of Jehovah's Witnesses.

_____ 17. Christian Science churches have no clergy.

_____ 18. As Christians we should think of Christian Scientists as closer to a cult than a sect.

C. Response to Christian Science

Work with others in your group to *outline* a letter of reply to Aunt Betty. Consider using the *Offense* approach (see back of your textbook) in answering these questions:

  1. What "offends" Aunt Betty about the Christian faith? How could we correct any misunderstandings she has about our faith?

  2. What real differences (offenses) exist between Christianity and Christian Science? What Scripture passages (or creeds) might we mention in support of the Christian stance?

Conclude by comparing your outlined letter to Response 2.

Holiness Church of God In Jesus' Name, Kingston, Georgia

CHALLENGE 3

SNAKE HANDLERS

Founding: In 1909 George Went Hensley, an evangelist of the Holiness Church, introduced snake handling into the Christian worship service. Basing the practice on Mark 16:17–18, Hensley convinced members of the congregation in Sale Creek, Tennessee, to "obey the Scriptures" and handle serpents.

Following: Today several scores of small groups in the US and Canada practice the rite (sacrament) of snake handling. Most of these congregations are members of the Holiness Church (although the majority in that denomination do not condone or accept this illegal practice).

Faith: The snake handlers believe the Bible is the infallible Word of God which must be understood and obeyed literally. And since Mark 16 says, "They will pick up serpents," those small congregations have incorporated snake handling into their worship services. Members pray, listen to guitar music, and dance as they encourage each other to pick up serpents—a sign of faith and of the presence of the Holy Spirit.

Handling snakes is always voluntary and is restricted to adolescents and adults. If bitten, handlers usually refuse medical treatment.

The snake handlers also believe:

*Regeneration and salvation are based on the vicarious, atoning death of Jesus Christ and come to the believer through the baptism of the Holy Spirit.

*Believers should earnestly seek the gifts of the Spirit which are proofs of salvation. These gifts include the five signs mentioned in Mark 16:17–18: "And these signs will accompany those who believe: in my name they will cast out demons; they will speak in new tongues; they will pick up serpents, and if they drink any deadly thing, it will not hurt them; they will lay their hands on the sick, and they will recover."

*Jesus' imminent second coming will bring everlasting life for the righteous and eternal damnation for the wicked.

*The existing social order is corrupt and utterly beyond redemption.

The following description of an actual event illustrates the amazing character of the snake handlers' activity:

July 1, 1973. The picnic was over and people were packing their things into their cars, when Clyde Ricker walked over to the plastic box with the sign on the side, "ONE BITE WILL KILL AN ELEPHANT." He slowly opened the door, reached inside and brought out the cobra that had been resting inside. After handling it for a while he put it inside of his shirt against his bare skin. After a short time he took it out and placed it around his neck. Then he held it in front of his face and kissed it. Soon his friend Lester Ball reached for the snake and Clyde let him take it. Before it was put back into the box, eight people held that snake in their hands. None of them was harmed. Afterward, the owner of the cobra, a professional snake exhibitor named John Wallis was heard to say, "I saw it, but I don't believe it. There's not enough money on the face of this earth to get me to do what they just did. They should have been bitten a dozen times. That cobra is after me all the time. I *know* he's vicious."

Robert W. Pelton and Karen W. Carden, *Snake Handlers,* p. 32

If I had planned to talk to Oscar Trumble about snakes, I would have brought my tape recorder. But I "just happened by," as they say, and just as accidentally got onto the subject. He was sitting, as he always does after supper, on his porch rocker, and he was in a talking mood. As near as I can recall, this is what he said . . .

For one thing I never handled no snakes till I was 'bout fourteen or fifteen. My brother held one onest when he was nine or ten, in a meetin' at the Holiness Church in Scrabble. When we got home from there he come right close to gettin' whupped. Daddy was gentle, but he just couldn't see as how a nine-year-old boy like Steven knowed for sure he was in the spirit.

Now that they've both gone on to glory and I think about it, I reckon he surely did know. Steven was like Daddy and I reckon they both knowed it. But Daddy still didn't want him startin' too young.

Before I taked up a serpent, I watched Daddy a hundred times I guess, maybe more. I usually knowed even before the singin' finished whether he'd be enough in the spirit to open that box. He'd take up any snake but always he'd start with his own. Plenty of snakes right around the floorboards or 'mongst the rocks by the creek. He'd only keep any one snake 'bout a month, then let it go and get another.

He'd wash the snake and shine him up nice 'fore takin' him to a service. Usually a big rattlesnake, 'bout four, five feet long. Put the box right under his seat in church and seem like he forgets all 'bout it.

But if the singin' gets goin' and lots of glory shoutin' and maybe guitars and tambourines, I'd see him shake just a bit and close his eyes. When he opened them, I knowed he'd pick up that snake. He was always in the spirit. He maybe handled five hundred different snakes and I 'member him serpent-bit three times and never sick to bed of it. But onest his arm swell up some.

I myself like to died the one time I got bit. I was twenty then and knowed when I was in the spirit or not. This time I wasn't but I was havin' a good time. I was feelin' the love of Jesus all 'round me and stampin'

I don't handle them every time. I really don't feel like it's necessary every time for me. But it does say, "They shall take up serpents." And Jesus is the one's doing the talking. Said, "They shall take them up." Well, I've got to do it, or somebody's got to do it, or else it makes Jesus out a liar, because if I tell you you shall go out that door, it means that you've got to go out there, one way or the other.

Elzie Preast.
Eleanor Dickinson and
Barbara Benziger, *Revival!*, p. 127

43

my feet and singin'—but I wasn't in the spirit. Always when I am, my fingers feel nothin' and my arms go cold. This time I felt joy in Jesus but my arms didn't get cold.

'Bout a half hour after I got bit, I thought I'd die. I couldn't hardly breathe and I was coughin' blood. I was cut to pieces, felt like—knowed I was dyin'. But the brothers and sisters kneeled 'round me and prayed direct to Jesus. And just as I knowed I was dyin', I got to know I would live. Couldn't move for a long time after I was so weak. But 'zackly when they touched me and prayed, I knowed Jesus done the healin' right then.

That's forty years past or so. Been handlin' snakes ever since, every week and more, but just when I'm filled with the Holy Ghost. I been bit more times than Daddy, maybe seven times, but never been so sick as that onest. Reckon Jesus had me bit to show the "doubting Thomases" that these here are real snakes with real poison. Else where's the true faith?

There's some look at us and shake their heads. Think we're crazy. But they don't know nothin' 'bout us. We do what we do 'cause the Bible tells us. It says in Mark 16 verse 18: "They shall take up serpents, and if they drink any deadly thing it shall not hurt them; they shall lay hands on the sick, and they shall recover."

Does it say *maybe* they shall take up serpents? No. Or if they *want* to they shall take up serpents? No. This is God's own Word we're talkin' of. You can't take it lightly. The *shalls* are 'bout serpents and layin' on hands. The drinkin' a deadly thing is an *if*; there ain't no command. So a man or woman's led to avoid poison, that's their own call. Myself, I don't drink strychnine. But I knowed it to be done and I seen it many times.

But I do take up serpents 'cause the Bible says *shall*. That there's a command. No doubt 'bout it. If I walk in the Lord, got to follow where he leads. Reckon that's to do what he says I *shall* do.

Lots of folks think we're crazies and call us "snakes." They think maybe we love snakes. But it's the Lord Jesus we love and no snakes. I'm afraid of snakes 'cause I ain't a fool. They can kill you. I'm not scared of death. Course I don't want to die. But I'm safe when

I'm in Jesus' will, and if he wants to take me to glory 'cause of a snake bite, I'll be ready to say Yes and Amen.

It's them others who've forsaken the Bible and most everythin' else. Schoolin' and money and clothes of today's kind is more important than obeyin' anythin' from God's Word.

But I see them and their kids. There's no respect; the kids leave the church behind and their salvation don't 'mount to nothin', 'cause they forsook the Word long before.

You don't see that here. We got good kids who respect their elders and dress decent. Even if you're old and unemployed like me, they respect you. And there's love 'tween us as there should be, 'cause it's the Holy Ghost who gives that love. If you see the brothers or sisters at James Hannah's Holiness Church kissin' each other with a holy kiss like the Bible says, don't ever think we're just puttin' on. We got somethin' the world don't know nothin' 'bout. The snakes is only a small part of it. The big thing is Jesus' own gift of the Holy Ghost. Ain't no one here goin' to be ashamed of that.

I knew that you all had something that I didn't have. And I realized that I wanted to have that, too. I wanted to be with the Spirit of God. Well, I went back to California. I got baptized there. But they don't have the Spirit there like they do here. Well, I've seen the power. I've seen the power and the work of Jesus and it's moved me to change my life. And I just wanted to thank you for my life, and to thank God that I'm alive and I can be here again.

Young man from California at
a Holiness Church meeting.
Eleanor Dickinson and Barbara Benziger,
Revival!, p. 131

FOR FURTHER READING

Dickinson, Eleanor and Barbara Benziger. *Revival!* New York: Harper & Row, 1974.

An illustrated interview of two Holy Ghost snake handlers.

Garino, David P. "Song, prayer, and snakes." *Wall Street Journal,* November 20, 1980.

Short but interesting article on the Holiness Church of Bob Fork, Kentucky.

LaBarre, Weston. *They Shall Take Up Serpents.* Minneapolis: University of Minnesota Press, 1962.

A psychological analysis with some description and history.

Photiadis, J. E., ed. *Religion in Appalachia.* Morgantown: West Virginia University for Extension and Continuing Education, 1978.

Has a chapter on "The Sacrament of Serpent-handling" by Mary Lee Daugherty. Explains why snake handling is so important to those who practice it. Good background detail on how these people live and worship.

First Strait Creek Holiness Church,
Rainsville, Alabama

SESSION GUIDE

CHALLENGE 3   SNAKE HANDLERS

A. Personal notes/questions on Challenge 3

B. Questions for discussion

　　1. What's your honest reaction to the snake handlers? Would you want to attend one of their services? Would you consider them Christians? Are they a sect or a cult?

　　2. Scripture study

　　　　a. "And these signs shall follow them who believe: In my name shall they cast out devils; they shall speak with new tongues; they shall take up serpents; and if they drink any deadly thing, it shall not hurt them; they shall lay hands on the sick, and they shall recover." (Mark 16:17–18, KJV)

　　　　　　The constant defense of any snake handler is simply to recite: "They *shall* take up serpents." Snake people believe they are obeying the Bible. How can we defend ourselves against the implied accusation that we don't obey Scripture?

　　　　b. What does the Bible say about "testing God"? Is snake handling a form of testing God, or is it more a testing of the believer? Explain.

c. In a well-known passage (Acts 28:1–6) Paul is bitten by a poisonous snake, shakes it off, and experiences no ill effects whatever. Isn't this a good argument for snake handling in general and for not seeking medical care if you are bitten while "in the spirit"? Explain.

d. Many Christians accept speaking in tongues as a special gift of the Spirit (it's mentioned along with snake handling in Mark 16:17–18). Why then don't we accept snake handling as a special gift of the Spirit? (See 1 Cor. 14:26–32.)

3. Most of us will never meet a snake handler, much less defend our faith to one. So why bother to learn about such a strange sect? What, if anything, can we learn from them?

Mormon Temple, Salt Lake City, Utah

MORMONS

Founding: The Church of Jesus Christ of Latter-day Saints is the official name of the religious group founded by Joseph Smith. Born in Sharon, Vermont, in 1805, Smith claimed to have received visions of a glorious messenger of God, Moroni. Moroni, Smith claimed, told him exactly where a book written on golden tablets was buried. In 1827 Smith unearthed the tablets and subsequently translated them into the *Book of Mormon,* a book which reveals how Christ visited the ancient Jewish inhabitants of the United States and gave them the gospel. In 1830 the Church of Jesus Christ of Latter-day Saints was officially organized in New York. When Smith died, the persecuted church moved west under the leadership of Brigham Young, finally settling in 1847 in Salt Lake Valley, Utah.

Following: Three fourths of the approximately 4.3 million Mormons reside in the United States, many of them near the capital or center of the religion, Salt Lake City, Utah. The Mormon community in Canada is concentrated around Cardston, Alberta, where another temple is located. According to *Time* magazine (8/7/78), Mormonism is the biggest, richest, strongest faith ever born on US soil; since World War II it has grown fourfold.

Faith: The Mormons accept several documents as authoritative for their faith: the Bible (insofar as it is translated correctly), the *Book of Mormon,* the *Doctrine and Covenants,* and *The Pearl of Great Price.*

Further revelations are received by the president of the office of High Priesthood. Based on these revelations, Mormons believe:

*"God was once as we are now, and is an exalted man" (Smith). God the Father and his Son, Jesus Christ, are distinct personalities, each possessing a physical body. God has a wife and produces spirit-children who are then united with the bodies of earthly children.

*Christ was the first spirit-child created by God the Father. Jesus practiced polygamy; he was the husband of Mary, Martha, and another Mary who became his wife at the wedding in Cana.

*When the kingdom of God is established in America, Jesus will be king. Christ died to free us from the consequences of Adam's sin (death), leaving us free to work for our own salvation. Christ saved people from the results of death, not from sin.

*The Holy Spirit, a separate God, works only in Mormons.

*Humans can become gods. Life is a probationary period; those who pass can go on to godhead. There are grades of salvation or exaltation: basically good non-Mormons go to the Terrestial Kingdom; outright sinners go to the Telestial Kingdom; Mormons who have done many good works go to the Celestial Kingdom. Those who have kept all of God's commandments become gods in the life to come.

*There is a priesthood—with clear ranks—for all "worthy" males.

*The church became apostate after Christ's time, but has now been restored by Smith and has the power to speak for God.

*Mission efforts must be vigorous. Mormon youth consider it an honor to be sent out by the church for two years of service as self-supporting missionaries.

*Since people have to learn how to become gods, education is important.

*A strong family life and honest business practices are essential for all Mormons who hope to be in the Celestial Kingdom.

*People who have died as non-Mormons can only have an opportunity to accept the "restored gospel" if Mormons on earth are baptized on their behalf in a temple (*Time,* 8/7/78). This accounts for the strong Mormon interest in genealogy.

It was a good meeting, I thought, blinking as I stepped out into the sunlight. The audience was double its usual size, and the guest preacher was unusually clear—he really let them have it. In fact, trying to reconstruct his main points must have slowed me down a bit; the bus was just pulling away when I turned the corner. A young woman about my age had missed it too. She stamped her foot, then shrugged and sat down on the bright green bench to wait. I knew I had seen her at the meeting.

"He really let them have it," I said as I walked up. She looked up and stared at me momentarily, then asked, "Have you ever talked to a Mormon?"

"No, not yet, but after hearing this lecture, I think I'd know what to say."

"This is your chance to try it out," she said, and smiled, though her eyes stayed serious. "The next bus doesn't come for twenty minutes."

"You're a Mormon?" I asked.

She nodded yes. "I saw the sign, 'The Mormon and How to Win Him,' so I went in to let him win me. But I'm pretty sure he lost. I'm still a Mormon."

I sat down beside her. "My name's Andrew," I said. "Are you angry about the lecture?"

She shrugged. "No, I guess not. I realize most other Christian churches won't give us the time of day. I do wish they'd present our teachings a bit more sympathetically."

"But look at the errors he documented!" I said.

She stared again. "Shall we really look at them?"

"You mean you have answers?"

"Let's begin with what he said about Joseph Smith. You tell me what you remember and let me react to that. I know that's not the method he suggested, but let's just talk instead of trying to convert each other."

"He didn't seem to think much of Smith," I said, trying to get my thoughts together. "Used words like 'ne'er-do-well' and said he spent his time looking for buried treasures before his so-called revelation."

"It was certainly negative. I suppose the point was that one can't expect the fairly ordinary, uneducated person to receive revelation from God. Had he wanted

What is a Mormon?
Strictly speaking, there is no such thing as a Mormon, and there is no Mormon Church. "Mormon" is merely a nickname for a member of the Church of Jesus Christ of Latter-day Saints.

Are Mormons Christians?
Unequivocally yes—both as to the name of the Church and in unqualified acceptance and worship of Jesus the Christ.

What do the Mormons believe about Jesus Christ?
They believe Him to be the Son of God, "the only begotten of the Father" in the flesh. They believe in His atoning sacrifice and literal resurrection. They accept Him as the Savior and Redeemer of mankind. They look to Him as the "one mediator between God and men" (1 Tim. 2:5), and pray to the Father in His name. They believe that He will come again and reign on earth (Acts 1:9–11).

Richard L. Evans, a member of the Council of Twelve of the Church of Jesus Christ of Latter-day Saints.
Leo Rosten, *Religions in America*, pp. 187, 198

to, though, your speaker could have found out that Joseph Smith grew up in an area of intense religious activity, that he had, as one Mormon writer puts it, 'an unwavering faith in God, a driving urge to find truth, a love for his fellow humans, a deep humility, and an inexhaustible capacity for obedience.' "

"But what about his education or lack of it?" I said.

"The writer I just quoted also said that Joseph Smith was 'practically unschooled.' To me, that's the best argument for taking his claims seriously. How could an uneducated, extremely ordinary young man compose a great document like the *Book of Mormon* in a matter of months? It's more difficult to believe he could make up all that information than to believe he received it through revelations from God. You certainly have to agree God may reveal himself to persons *we* would hardly choose. That's why no one believed the apostle Paul at first."

"Okay," I said, "I'll drop the attack on Joseph Smith, though I still think he's a phony. The really significant point made today was that Joseph Smith's revelations don't agree with the Bible. I don't see how anyone could avoid admitting that."

"It depends on what you mean by 'agreeing with the Bible.' If you mean agreeing with what you or the different Christian churches think is the meaning of the Bible, then it's not surprising you find that our *revelations* disagree with some of your teachings. But what if your understanding of the meaning of the Bible was incomplete?"

"How could that be?" I asked. "Christians have been studying the Bible for about fifteen hundred years."

"And in those years, what's happened?" she said. "For every question raised about the nature of God, Jesus Christ, or the soul, the various churches argued various ways—proving they could not agree. They gradually lost the simple, direct faith of the apostles that Jesus himself taught. They were really in need of a revelation."

"But revelation stopped with the last book of the Bible," I argued.

"More likely John was warning future writers not to change or add to his book of Revelation, if that's what you're talking about. No one in Jesus' time could have known of a specific set of books called the Bible. And why would you believe revelation has stopped? The words that led Joseph Smith to pray for revelation were from James 1:5: 'If any of you lack wisdom, let him ask God, who gives to all men generously and without reproaching, and it will be given him.' Don't you believe God means what he says? We believe strongly that revelation still takes place. Otherwise we might be unable to receive the wisdom we need for today."

I remembered something the speaker had said. "But how about the polygamy revelation?" I asked. "How can one revelation contradict another?"

"His presentation was a bit one-sided," she said quietly. "It's more complicated than that. First of all, one must recognize that there was a time when the Old Testament Jews were permitted to have more than one wife. Later it became inappropriate for them to be polygamous, so monogamy became the revealed standard."

"But if that's so, how could one justify going back to polygamy?"

"I prefer to call it plural marriage, since for Mormons this marriage involved sacred obligations. At the time plural marriage was practiced, there *was* a need for it: the church had to grow rapidly so its people could help settle the American West. Plural marriage was finally abandoned after a long struggle between the church and the US government. However, the revelation of President Woodruff was not that plural marriage was wrong, but that the members of the Church of the Latter-day Saints should not contract marriages forbidden by the law of the land. That's not much different from Paul's advice that Jewish bishops in a Roman world should only have one wife."

"I guess the speaker would have had a reply to that. Unfortunately, I don't. But let's talk about the Mormon teaching that God the Father has a body. The Bible says God is a Spirit. How can one defend the idea of God having arms, or—"

[The] pattern of the incidence of the revelations, as well as the scope of their content, gives credibility to the Mormon claim that this was a purposeful program operated in accordance with the will of the Lord, and not one used by Joseph Smith to further his own purposes, impress his hearers, or satisfy his own vanity or ambitions.

Wallace F. Bennett, *Why I Am a Mormon*, p. 253

I am a Mormon because I was born of Mormon parents into a Mormon home.

I have remained a Mormon because I have found spiritual, intellectual, and social satisfaction in my membership.

These answers might be reason enough. But there are more. I am a Mormon because all that I have learned in the Church and all that I have experienced because of it have brought the unshakeable assurance that this plan and program are of God. Through my membership and participation in the Church's program, my family and I have been protected, healed, and blessed. In seeking to live by its principles, we have been given faith in their divinity. For us, it is the true church of Christ, and we are humbly proud to be called "Mormons."

Wallace F. Bennett, *Why I Am a Mormon*, p. 252

"But you yourself can quote Jesus as saying 'into your hands I commend my Spirit.' And you will read the phrase, 'Give ear, O Lord.' Either you can be like the Greek world—which heavily influenced Christian thinking—and say God is only Spirit and thus we are not much like him, or you can emphasize that we are *truly* created in God's image. The revelations about God's body help us come closer to God. He is our Father and we are his children. Through Christ we can be like him. One writer has said, 'As God is, man may become.' "

"We've got a few minutes left before the bus comes," I said, knowing I was not getting very far. "And you've just mentioned Christ. The Bible teaches that he is the way, the truth, the life. Salvation is found only in him. Yet you teach salvation by works."

"At least that was the speaker's story."

"Wasn't it true?"

"Hardly. Humanity without Christ is dead. And through Christ we are saved from death. 'There is no other name'—I'm sure you know the text. But you know too that 'faith without works is dead.' Unfortunately the Bible provided very little information about human existence either before or after mortal life. This was another area where additional revelation was needed, sought, and received. Now we know that we take the results of our actions in this life into eternity; that gives each of our days far more significance than if we had no idea of the meaning of our actions."

"Is that why you stress moral behavior so much?"

"Perhaps, although celestial marriage is also important because it teaches eternal value. If you examine our faith, you'll see that the basic revelations have tremendous practical value for each day of the Mormon's life."

I looked at my watch. "The bus'll be here in a minute, and I transfer at the second stop. This has been good for me, but I've got to rethink the speech and maybe do some homework." I hesitated because she was already extracting a pen from her purse.

"I'm Paula Richards, and you're going to ask me for my phone number," she said, smiling. "And no, I'm

58

not offended. But I should warn you, I'm new in town. I've come here as the last stop in my ministry, and I've got a string of converts."

"I'll do my homework," I said. "I'm no missionary, but it'd be kind of nice to have a convert to claim." I took the slip of paper she held out and put it in my shirt pocket.

That was two days ago. I'd like to call her, but I'm guessing she's got books on my faith. I've got one or two on hers, but I'm pretty sure she can answer what's in them. So where do I go from here?

FOR FURTHER READING

Anderson, Einar. *Inside Story of Mormonism.* Grand Rapids, Mich.: Kregel Publications, 1973.

A former Mormon explains the history and teachings of Mormonism.

Bennett, Wallace F. *Why I Am a Mormon.* New York: Thomas Nelson and Sons, 1958.

Hoekema, Anthony A. *The Four Major Cults.* Grand Rapids, Mich.: Wm. B. Eerdmans Pub. Co., 1974.

Contains an eighty-seven-page chapter on Mormonism. Thorough, scholarly, biblical. Often referred to by other writers. All chapters of *The Four Major Cults* are also available as separate paperback books (Eerdmans, 1973).

Kaiser, Edgar. *How to Respond to the Latter-day Saints.* St. Louis: Concordia, 1977.

Short but excellent overview.

Martin, Walter R. *The Maze of Mormonism.* Santa Ana, Calif.: Vision House Publishers, 1978.

Billed as "the very best reference on Mormonism compared to Christianity." Written by an evangelical, Christian scholar.

"Mormonism Enters New Era," *Time,* August 7, 1978.

Interesting, illustrated article focusing on Mormon president Spencer W. Kimball's revelation to allow blacks into the priesthood. Much general information too.

Ropp, Harry. *The Mormon Papers.* Downers Grove, Ill.: Inter-Varsity Press, 1977.

Mostly a discussion of the Mormon scriptures, but also includes a section on witnessing to Mormons.

Rosten, Leo. *Religions of America.* New York: Simon and Schuster, 1975.

Richard L. Evans answers questions about the Mormon Church (pp. 186–99).

Smith, Joseph. *Book of Mormon.* Salt Lake City: Church of Jesus Christ of Latter-day Saints, 1952.

Mormon missionaries hand out free copies of this one.

——————. *Doctrine and Covenants.* Salt Lake City: Church of Jesus Christ of Latter-day Saints, 1952.

——————. *The Pearl of Great Price.* Salt Lake City: Church of Jesus Christ of Latter-day Saints, 1952.

CASSETTE TAPES

Martin, Walter. *The Maze of Mormonism* (C-40) and *Who Really Wrote the Book of Mormon?* (C-96). Available from the Christian Research Institute, Box 500, San Juan Capistrano, California 92693. Write for current brochure and prices.

FILMS

According to Christian Schools International, Mormon missionaries are willing to show these films free of charge:

Man's Search for Happiness. Brigham Young University, 1964. "This film gives the Mormon view of where we came from, why we are here, and where we go after death." Color. 14 minutes.

Meet the Mormons. Brigham Young University, 1973. "This film introduces the non-Mormon to the Mormon Church and its activities." Color. 24 minutes.

Joseph Smith

SESSION GUIDE

CHALLENGE 4   MORMONS

A. Personal notes/questions on Challenge 4

B. A major question for discussion

Are Mormons Christians? Support your answer with specific references to Paula's comments and other material in Challenge 4.

C. Our response to Mormons

Look over the five apologetic methods described at the back of your textbook. Which of the five do you think would be best when talking with Mormons like Paula? Explain your choice and briefly outline the direction it could take.

D. For additional discussion

What can we learn from the Mormons?

Ellen G. White

SEVENTH-DAY ADVENTISTS

Founding: In the 1800s a group called the Adventists believed William Miller's prediction that Christ would return in 1844. When the year passed with no second coming, Adventists were disappointed and disillusioned. They couldn't figure out what had gone wrong.

But Ellen Gould White (1827–1915) knew. White, a devout Adventist, had a number of visions explaining the "great disappointment" of 1844. One particular vision emphasized the restoration of the Sabbath to the seventh day.

Soon many frustrated Adventists were listening to Ellen White. And out of her visions, prophecies, and writings, a new church was formed—the Seventh-day Adventists. In 1863 the first general conference of SDA was held in Battle Creek, Michigan.

Following: Recent statistics show 28,000 members in 240 churches in Canada and 556,000 in 3,667 churches in the United States. Worldwide membership is roughly two and a half million, with three and a half million in Sabbath school. Forty-four SDA publishing houses produce 385 periodicals in 225 languages. The Seventh-day Adventists run 230 hospitals and 5,000 schools and colleges. They have more missionaries than any other denomination except the Methodists and are known for their large contributions to their churches.

Faith: *Saturday, not Sunday, is observed as the Sabbath. In the beginning, God set aside the seventh day of the week, not the first. The fourth commandment says to remember the Sabbath day. Christ, our example, observed the seventh-day Sabbath (Luke 23:56). "There is not a single text in the Bible suggesting that Christ authorized a change of the Sabbath from the seventh day to the first" (Arthur S. Maxwell, quoted in "What Is a Seventh-day Adventist?" *Relgions of America* by Leo Rosten, p. 244).

*Christ is coming soon (Adventism). Seventh-day Adventists emphasize Christ's words: "When ye shall see these things come to pass, know that it is nigh, even at the doors" (Mark 13:29). Moral collapse, great fear and confusion, and unprecedented increase of knowledge are all signs of the times.

*Since 1844 Christ has been conducting an investigative judgment in heaven, reviewing the cases of all believers to see if they are worthy of eternal life. When he's finished, he will return to claim his own and reign with them for one thousand years in heaven (the millennium). Then the final judgment will take place; the earth will be renewed and will become the eternal home of the faithful.

*The Seventh-day Adventists are the remnant church, chosen by God to bear the gospel and usher in the return of Christ. However, God has a precious remnant in every church.

*The Bible is the inspired Word of God; it alone is authoritative. According to a 1975 book giving advice to SDA preachers: "After the Bible, our other primary source is the writings of Ellen G. White. These writings are without peer when it comes to illuminating and amplifying the Scriptures" (C. Bradford, *Preaching to the Times,* p. 39).

*Adventists accept the traditional Christian teachings on the virgin birth, the Trinity, the deity of Jesus Christ, and salvation by grace alone.

*Baptism (by immersion) and communion (preceded by the foot-washing rite) are sacraments.

*Since our bodies are temples of the Spirit, we must avoid meat, alcohol, tobacco, and other harmful indulgences.

Dad and Mom, I know I'm agitated and upset, and I *know* I'm talking above a whisper, but I'm trying as hard as I can to keep a certain calm about me. We've handled lots of disagreements before, and you've been great. But I know this is upsetting you far more than it upsets me. So I'm asking that you let me say everything I've got to say without stopping me. If you can do that, I'll try to be quiet while you have your say too. That way we can sit in this restaurant without attracting attention and still be ready for Bob when he comes.

He'll be here in an hour, and he plans to ask your permission to marry me. In fact, we'd like more than your permission: we'd like your love and blessing as well. But we know how upsetting it has been to you that Bob is Seventh-day Adventist.

At first I was bothered by our religious differences too. I believed that the SDA was one of the cults, that they denied important aspects of Christian belief. But, partly through Bob, and partly through my own study, I've concluded that though in the past the SDA often behaved like a cult, its official statements and the lives of its members both demand that I accept them as one of the mainline churches. Bob is deeply involved in his church life and I don't want to interfere with that. In fact, I want to be a part of it. After we marry, I intend to join Bob's congregation and become a Seventh-day Adventist.

Please don't get upset; let me continue. When I first began dating Bob, you brought me two special concerns about the SDA. You described the church as a cult because they practiced Sabbath worship and because they accepted the writings of Ellen G. White as prophetic. You attacked them for their emphasis on Christ's imminent return and for what you called their legalism. I've thought about these concerns. I'd like to say a bit about each.

Let me start with Ellen G. White. Seventh-day Adventists believe she received the gift of prophecy and that her visions and writings are a light upon Scripture. That's all. In fact, the church's official documents state that the writings of Ellen G. White, like all other writings and teachings, must be judged

A Seventh-day Adventist is one who, having accepted Christ as his personal Savior, walks in humble obedience to the will of God as revealed in the Holy Scriptures. A Bible-loving Christian, he seeks to pattern his life according to the teachings of this book, while looking for the imminent return of the Lord.

Arthur S. Maxwell, "What Is a Seventh-day Adventist?" *Religions of America*, p. 245

An unspeakable awe filled me, that I, so young and feeble, should be chosen as the instrument by which God would give light to his people.

Ellen G. White, *Testimonies for the Church VI*, p. 62

by the Bible—that the Bible is *never* to be judged by those writings. Sounds a lot like the way we revere the works of Calvin or Luther or Knox, doesn't it?

Of course, some members of the SDA don't follow these official teachings as closely as I'd like—but isn't that true of all churches? The point of all this is that I want you to understand that your daughter can join the Seventh-day Adventists and still maintain her faith in the Bible as God's holy inspired Word and in the major doctrines of Christianity: the Seventh-day Adventists accept the Trinity, the virgin birth, and the deity and Lordship of Jesus. So you see, as far as doctrines go, the SDA cannot be grouped with cults like the Jehovah's Witnesses or Christian Science.

True, the Adventist position on Sabbath worship is certainly different from our church's position. While we worship on Sunday in commemoration of Christ's resurrection, the Adventists continue to gather on the seventh day, on Saturday. Why? Because they cannot find a text in the Bible describing Christ's authorization for changing the Sabbath to Sunday.

As a result their interpretation of Sabbath observance has become an important part of their tradition. But they *don't* claim—as some suggest—that those who worship on Sunday will not be saved. Ellen White once said, "There are true Christians in every church, not excepting the Roman Catholic communion, who honestly believe that Sunday is the Sabbath of divine appointment. God accepts their sincerity of purpose and their integrity before him."

As to their emphasis on Christ's return—certainly this is important to the SDA. They *do* preach that Christ's return is imminent. They put far more emphasis on it than our own church does. And I'm sure we would not agree with some of the more intricate explanations they put forth regarding just how that return will be carried out. But please remember that they differ from most of the earlier Adventist movements too. Unlike Miller's followers, the Seventh-day Adventists don't set specific dates for Christ's return. They *do* believe that return will be soon—the signs of our age point in that direction—but they don't name a specific year or month.

Instead they focus on living in the awareness of Christ's coming. And I've discovered that's really a positive way to live. They set their eyes on eternal rather than material goals, and they rely—in a very real way—on Christ's saving work.

That's right—for the SDA it *is* Christ's work that saves us. In 1970 the General Conference of the Seventh-day Adventists said:

> ...The law cannot save the transgressor from his sin, nor impart power to keep him from sinning. In infinite love and mercy God provided a way whereby this may be done. He furnishes a substitute, even Christ the righteous one, to die in man's stead, making "him to be sin for us, who knew no sin; that we might be made the righteousness of God in him" (2 Cor. 5:21). We are justified, not by obedience to the law, but by the grace that is in Christ Jesus.
>
> [See Appendix III fundamental beliefs of SDA in 1970.]

This certainly is not legalism. I know you believe that the SDA has made the observance of the fourth commandment and other works conditional for salvation. But, although the SDA does teach that at present Christ is carrying out an investigation of each person's works, they insist this does *not* mean a person is saved by what he or she has done. Perhaps our own church could often be described as having a similar problem. We know "faith without works is dead" and yet we insist it is through faith alone that we become right with God.

What I'm saying is this: perhaps you won't be satisfied that the SDA is entirely accurate on every point it proclaims. But if you examine its teachings, you must agree that officially its stands are explicitly and clearly Christian. When you add to that its solid reputation for encouraging a clean-living, health-conscious lifestyle, its solid emphasis on Christian education and mission work, you must be ready to forgive its emergence from a cult-like past, and you must be ready to accept that your daughter can be both a Christian and a member of the Seventh-day Adventist Church.

SDA members are selfless in their devotion and loyal to its creed and propagation. There is personal sacrifice in giving and service that is altogether astonishing. The expansion of their movement is phenomenal. . .and worldwide. Their members are honorable and lovable in the main.

An ex-SDA.
Edmond Gruss, *Cults and the Occult in the Age of Aquarius*, p. 63

FOR FURTHER READING

Hoekema, Anthony A. *The Four Major Cults*. Grand Rapids, Mich.: Wm. B. Eerdmans Pub. Co., 1963.

In a thorough and scholarly chapter, Hoekema argues that Adventism is a cult. All chapters of *The Four Major Cults* are also available as separate paperback books (Eerdmans, 1973).

Liberty. Religious Liberty Association of America and the Seventh-day Adventist Church, the Herald and Review Publishing Association.

An excellent, bimonthly journal "dedicated to the preservation of religious freedom, advocating no political or economic theories." Sparkling journalism; interesting topics.

Martin, Walter R. *The Kingdom of the Cults*. Minneapolis: Bethany Fellowship, Inc., 1965.

While critical of some Adventist teachings, Martin argues that the Adventists are not a cult.

Numbers, Ronald. *Prophetess of Health: Ellen G. White*. New York: Harper & Row, 1976.

An interesting look at the founder of the Seventh-day Adventists.

Rosten, Leo. *Religions of America*. New York: Simon and Schuster, 1975.

Includes a chapter of basic questions and answers by Arthur S. Maxwell, outstanding SDA author and editor.

The Sabbath Commandment

זָכוֹר֙ אֶת־י֣וֹם הַשַּׁבָּ֖ת לְקַדְּשֽׁוֹ

Remember the Sabbath day, to keep it holy.

Exodus 20:8

SESSION GUIDE

CHALLENGE 5   SEVENTH-DAY ADVENTISTS

A. Personal notes/questions on Challenge 5

B. Defending your views

Points of difference do exist between SDA and us—differences which have caused some orthodox and evangelical Christians to call SDA a cult, but differences which SDA defends.

If an SDA asked you why you reject some of the things they believe so strongly, would you be able to adequately explain and justify our own position on these points? To be specific, what would you say to a Seventh-day Adventist who

1. wants to know why your church worships on Sunday, the first day of the week, instead of on the Sabbath (seventh day) as the Bible so clearly commands?

2. asks why you think it's OK to respect Calvin and Luther, but have questions about the way they respect Ellen G. White?

3. asks why your church doesn't preach that Christ will soon return and the world will end (Adventism)?

Use the space below for notes:

C. If you were Anne's parents, how would you react to her plans to marry a Seventh-day Adventist?

_____ Welcome the marriage. The man Anne is marrying may believe somewhat differently on minor points, but his basic beliefs are thoroughly Christian.

_____ Oppose the marriage. Anne would be marrying someone outside the Christian church, more a cult member than a fellow believer.

_____ Other?

Compare your answer with Response 5.

Victor Paul Wierwille

CHALLENGE 6

THE WAY

Founding: In 1968 Victor Paul Wierwille, a former minister of the United Church of Christ, founded The Way in New Knoxville, Ohio. Wierwille, who claims to have done the only "pure and correct" interpretation of the Bible since the first century, explains his views in *Jesus Christ Is NOT God* and other books. The Way was begun as a "biblical research" organization (it claims that it is not a church) and was designed to teach "abundant living" to its followers.

Following: Since Wierwille keeps no records, estimates of membership are somewhat vague. Appealing mostly to comfortable middle- or upper-class families, The Way is tightly organized along the model of a *tree*. The tree *roots* are the international headquarters in New Knoxville. The *trunk* is the complex of national organizations (The Way has followers in close to thirty-five different countries of the world). The *limb* is the state organizations (fifty at last count). The *branch* is the city organization. The *twig* is the local fellowship or Way group. The *leaves* are the individual followers of The Way, of whom there are about 20,000 (Jack Sparks, *The Mindbenders*). Followers of The Way appear to be concentrated mostly in the north central United States and to be spreading out from there. Much of their work is done on high school and college campuses.

Faith: *Jesus is not God. According to Wierwille, Jesus is the Son of God but not God the Son. "Show me one place in the Bible where it says Jesus is God," Wierwille challenges. Christ did not exist prior to his conception in Mary's womb. At his baptism he received a human holy spirit which enabled him to do his work. The most important thing Christ did was not dying on the cross or rising from the dead or ascending into heaven (though he did in fact do all these), but giving his followers the human holy spirit. Thus, although Christ is our Lord and even our Savior, he is not God.

*There is no Trinity. Christ is not God. The Holy Spirit is the same as God, not a distinct person in the Trinity. This Holy Spirit (God) gave the human holy spirit as a gift to people on Pentecost and today.

*All believers must receive the human holy spirit and speak in tongues.

*"Salvation is only a legal transaction secured by the death and resurrection of Christ. Salvation is experienced by gaining the right knowledge, offered by various Bible study courses of The Way" (Jack Sparks, *The Mindbenders*, p. 217).

*The Bible is the inspired Word of God, but only the epistles of Paul—and maybe Acts—apply to Christians today. The teachings of Dr. Wierwille are necessary to correctly understand the Bible.

80

Excerpt From Clare's Diary

September 5

Dear Diary,

I'm writing to you because I want to think some of this through before I talk to anyone about it. Mom and Dad will never understand. Mom will just say, "But that isn't what the church teaches," and get angry if I don't accept her argument as final. And Dad will back her up as usual. Besides, as you and I both know, the church really does not teach the things I've been learning the past few days. If someone accused me of being interested in a sect or cult, I'd have a hard time defending myself.

Still, there are several reasons I'm interested in The Way, and if I can say them clearly to you, perhaps I'll be able to say them clearly to Mom and Dad.

First is this matter of understanding the Bible. I've been as faithful as anyone I know in church school classes—remember how excited I was when I got the sixth-year memory work award? But two weeks ago I was forced to realize that I really don't understand some important parts of the Bible's message. I couldn't defend them at all.

I just happened to meet Phil at a gas station in Toronto. At the time I was pretty open to any help I could get—a flat tire on the outer exchanges of highway 401 would unnerve a truckdriver, not to mention a smalltown girl like me. The tire had to be ordered from some other station, and I had an hour or two to kill. Phil was just picking up his car. He said he was from St. Catharines and he knew a bunch of people from my high school—so I took a chance on lunch.

The whole lunch became a sort of church school "nightmare," though nightmares ought not to be fun. Here I am out with a really sweet guy who seems to have the world by the tail. But in his car I picked up the book *Jesus Christ Is NOT God* by the founder of The Way. It sounded like a terrible title, and I told Phil so. And that became the topic for the whole lunch.

I guess I lost the argument because I couldn't explain the Trinity at all. Phil showed clearly how the whole idea of three-in-one came from pagan religions

For years I did nothing but read around the Word of God. I used to read two or three theological works weekly for month after month and year after year. I knew what professor so-and-so said, what Dr. so-and-so and the Right Reverend so-and-so said, but I could not quote you The Word. I had not read it. One day I finally became so disgusted and tired of reading around The Word *that I hauled over 3,000 volumes of theological works to the city dump. I decided to quit reading around* The Word. *Consequently I have spent years studying* The Word—*its integrity, its meaning, its words.*

Victor Wierwille, *Power for Abundant Living,* pp. 119–20

They were rattling off Bible passages so fast that you couldn't check them. They finally said, "Don't try to look things up, just listen...." In their study sessions they teach that you can't trust the Bible.... They would add sentences.... They would tell you to cross out entire passages.

Former Way follower.
Tempe (Ariz.) *Daily News,*
Saturday, February 7, 1981

Since we are sons of God and Jesus Christ is the Son of God, we are, as it says in Hebrews, his brothers. Being brothers of Jesus Christ, we are now on legal par with him.

Jesus was not and is not God; neither are we: but we are heirs of God and joint-heirs with Christ. Furthermore Jesus Christ is also our redeemer and our lord. He is the Son of God. *We would say if questioned by Jesus as his disciples were, "But whom say ye that I am?"* Thou art the Christ, the Son of the living God.

Victor Wierwille, *Jesus Christ Is NOT God*, p. 55

When Thomas exclaimed, "My Lord and my God" (John 20:28), he was observing the resurrected Christ as "my godly Lord." The word "lord" expresses the fact and the word "godly" intensifies "lord" to the superlative degree. Indeed, my godly Lord is exactly what Jesus Christ is!

Victor Wierwille, *Jesus Christ Is NOT God*, p. 35

and was added to Christianity by the Emperor Constantine. I kept trying to point to verses about Father, Son, and Holy Ghost, but I really couldn't think of very many.

Anyway, when I finally admitted I couldn't defend the Trinity, Phil said that was good. He told me the next step was to see that Jesus had to be completely separate from God in order to be his only Son. He claimed that if Jesus had been God, he couldn't have made payment for our sin; and he read me a line from the book that said Jesus "had to be a lamb from the flock."

I was amazed when Phil went on to explain that Jesus was still our redeemer. But he could defend that too. What impressed me was that he could defend *everything* he said by referring to Scripture. He explained how the words *Holy Spirit* have two separate meanings: one when they refer to God and another when they refer to the human holy spirit he gives us when we are "born of the spirit."

By the time Phil brought me back to pick up my car, I had agreed to visit his twig which was meeting that evening. I thought I knew what to expect: people always warned me that the cults get you and brainwash you and force you to sort of accept out of desperation. But the twig meeting wasn't like that. Everyone was really glad to see me and to know I was interested. They never pushed me at all. Some of them started talking in tongues, which would have seemed ridiculous to me under most circumstances. But other members could interpret what the spirit was saying through those tongues, and it really made sense. One of the things they were saying was how grateful to God they were that the truth was being revealed so that it could really be used in our lives.

I could see that this group had two things I was looking for: answers to the really hard questions about the Bible and an inside experience to testify that they were born again.

Since The Way is more a Bible research and study organization than a church, I don't think I went against the church by signing up for the first course. Anyway, it's twelve sessions of three hours each for eighty-five dollars. That's less than two dollars an hour, so no one can say I'm being cheated. I've only been to one session so far and discovered it's mainly a videotaped lecture by Dr. Wierwille, the preacher who began The Way. You don't take notes or anything, but at the end you can ask questions. So far I don't have questions to ask. I was impressed by how many answers he had to questions I wouldn't have thought *had* answers—and how he uses Scripture all the time.

Already I feel that I've got more energy and enthusiasm for being a Christian than I ever had before. I think it's because I'm losing my doubts. I never could understand the Trinity or Christ's divinity. To have these questions completely settled by a correct interpretation of Scripture is really exciting. To study the Bible with enthusiastic people and then to find that enthusiasm rubbing off on me is a great experience.

I think I'll leave Mom and Dad in the dark for a while yet. After all, it's not as if I'm joining a commune or anything like that. So it'll just be you and me, diary, for now at least—until I finish the P.F.A.L. course. Then, if it works as I think it will, I ought to be able to handle anyone.

In the beginning was the Word (God) and the (revealed) Word was with God (with Him in His fore-knowledge, yet independent of Him), and the Word was God.

John 1:1, rewritten by Victor Wierwille.
Victor Wierwille, *Jesus Christ Is NOT God,* p. 35

FOR FURTHER READING

Enroth, Ronald. *Youth, Brainwashing, and the Extremist Cults.* Grand Rapids, Mich.: Zondervan, 1977.

In a short chapter (10 pages), tells the fascinating story of one person who joined The Way. Exposes the brainwashing techniques used by this cult.

Sparks, Jack. *The Mindbenders.* Nashville: Thomas Nelson Inc., 1977.

Introduces the history and theology of The Way in a chapter of about thirty pages. Also includes method of operations and a refutation.

Wierwille, Victor. *Jesus Christ Is NOT God.* New Knoxville, Ohio: The American Christian Press, 1975.

CASSETTE TAPES

Walter, Martin. *The New Cults: the Way.* C-78. Available from the Christian Research Institute, Box 500, San Juan Capistrano, California 92693. Write for current prices and free brochure.

Victor Paul Wierwille, Founder of "The Way"

SESSION GUIDE

CHALLENGE 6   THE WAY

A. Personal notes/questions on Challenge 6

B. The Way and Christ

1. The most important question we can ask of any religious group is, "What do you believe about Jesus Christ?" Review The Way's teaching about Christ. Then see what you can do with Wierwille's challenge:

SHOW ME ONE PLACE IN THE BIBLE WHERE IT SAYS JESUS IS GOD.

2. Is the matter of Christ's divinity ultimately a matter of faith, something for which we will never find biblical proof? Explain.

C. Our response

1. What does The Way offer to people like Clare who "could never understand the Trinity or Christ's divinity"?

2. Do you think most Christians have doubts about these doctrines at some time or another? If so, how should they handle their doubts and unanswered questions?

3. If and when Clare tells her parents about her involvement with The Way, they should:

_____ a. have her deprogrammed by a professional, realizing that nothing they say will make any difference anyway.

_____ b. listen to her, then attempt to show her that Wierwille is a poor Bible scholar, a typical cultic leader who has departed from the traditional Christian interpretations of the Scripture (*Test of Tradition* approach).

_____ c. have an open and friendly discussion with Clare. Find out why The Way attracts her and Christianity doesn't. Attempt to show her that Christianity supplies all the "answers" we really *need* to know and that some doctrines will always be wrapped in mystery. Assure her that doubt is not her unique problem, that every Christian needs to grow in faith (*Need-Nourishment* approach).

_____ d. listen to Clare's explanations but don't attempt to argue or convince her. Just pray she'll come to her senses and recognize The Way as the unbiblical cult it is.

_____ e. Other?

Hutterite Community, Rifton, New York

CHALLENGE 7

HUTTERITES

Founding: The first Hutterite colony was founded in Moravia in 1528 by an Anabaptist minister named Jacob Hutter. When Hutter was burned at the stake, Peter Rideman took over the leadership and wrote the Hutterite *Confession of Faith.* Fiercely persecuted in Europe because of their pacificism and indifferent attitude toward government, the Hutterites fled to the western prairies of the United States in the 1870s. During World War I, draft laws and anti-German feeling in the United States led many Hutterites to move to Alberta, Saskatchewan, and Manitoba.

Following: In 1979 there were approximately 16,000 Hutterites in Canada and 9,000 in the United States (living in 250 colonies of up to 150 persons in each). Although anyone is welcome to join the church after living in the colony for a year and being baptized, only nineteen adults have joined the Hutterites during the last four decades. At the same time fewer than 2 percent leave permanently. Growth of the colonies comes from very large families (11 to 12 children in the past; now closer to 8 to 9 per family).

Faith: *"Our colony...is like a spiritual ark. Here, no one is in need. Everyone helps in the work, according to ability. We believe in glorifying God through hard work and a simple life. Our ways are based on the book of Acts, chapter 2, verses 44 and 45: 'And all that believed were together, and had all things common; And sold their possessions and goods, and parted them to all men, as every man had need."

Hutterite preacher, quoted in William Albert Allard,
"The Hutterites, Plain People of the West,"
National Geographic, July 1970, pp. 102–3

*Every member "shall give and devote all his or her time, labor, services, earnings, and energies to the community, freely, voluntarily, and without compensation."

Constitution of the Hutterite Brethren Church

*Because of sin, people are prone to be individualistic, but it is the community's job to protect members from self-centeredness, to develop *gelassenheit* (giving-up-ness), which implies submitting one's whole nature to God's will.

*The world is evil and corrupt, concerned with pleasure...therefore removed from God and to be avoided. Hutterite homes do without TV and radio. Clothing is austere: men wear black denim trousers with suspenders; women wear ankle-length skirts, aprons, long hair. Members refuse to hold civic office or join the military, but do pay their taxes. And modern technology is freely used (electricity, farm equipment, etc.) as long as it meets group approval and is profitable to the colony. Buying and selling contacts with the outside world are inevitable, but deliberately limited.

*Adult baptism is the way of officially joining the colony. Leaders in the church (males only, headed by an unordained preacher) are leaders in the colony and make the key decisions. Church services are held daily and include much singing. The church does not support mission work.

*The Hutterites accept most basic Christian beliefs (deity of Christ, salvation by grace, etc.).

Dear Thomas,

You will probably read this just before supper time. I know you won't look at the kitchen table before that. By then the bus will be in Moose Jaw, and I'll be an hour or two from the colony.

I suppose you will be surprised and disappointed. Disappointed because I'll miss your wedding and never meet your family. Surprised that I would finally have chosen to leave the city for the life I swore I would never return to—that dull, quiet colony!

After two years in Regina, I can't deny having enjoyed it. Last week we did some electrical repairs on the eighth floor of an office building where I could look over the water to the government houses. It was beautiful; Waldeck and Moose Jaw have nothing by comparison. But it's not the beautiful parts of the city I want to flee. It's the ugly loneliness of the life I'm living. No Hutterite need be lonely, and that's one reason I'm going back.

It's not just that I need to feel "at home again," but that I realize I don't know how to value myself apart from my home. When I made my first trip to Moose Jaw with four of my brothers—all of us dressed the same—I knew outsiders thought us strange. But it didn't bother me then. I knew how much I was a part of my community. Later, when we went to town to buy parts or special feeds, I always tried to slip away and page through some adventure magazines or, if there was time, see a movie. By the time I was fifteen I was privately learning the sort of English I knew I would need to go out and "see for myself." When I finally confessed my desires to my German teacher, he understood completely. It was with his permission and the preacher's that I came to Regina. Though I had no provisional certificate, I had as much mechanical training as most apprentices would be expected to have—at the colony everyone knows their trades. I had no trouble getting a job.

I had been here a year when you advertised for a roommate. Remember your surprise when I told you I was, in your words, "a Hoot"? You didn't believe it, and there were times I hardly did myself. But under-

If a boy tells me he wants to leave, I tell him to go ahead, give it a whirl. See if it's better on the outside.

John Stahl, preacher.
William Albert Allard,
"The Hutterites, Plain People of the West,"
National Geographic, July 1970

I saw a lot of the world. And I met a lot of different kinds of people. But I found that this is the only way for me to live. The big cities, the way people fight and kill each other... that's not for me.

Martin Stahl, a Hutterite who returned to the colony
after seven years on the outside.
William Albert Allard, "The Hutterites,
Plain People of the West,"
National Geographic, July 1970

We bring up our children in the divine discipline and teach them from the beginning to know God. But we permit them not to go to other schools, since there they teach but the wisdom, art, and practices of the world, and are silent about divine things.

Peter Rideman, *Confession of Faith*, p. 130

Community, however, is naught else than that those who have fellowship have all things in common together, none having aught for himself, but each having all things with the others.

Peter Rideman, *Confession of Faith*, p. 92

neath my skills at playing the city boy's part, a battle was going on. A battle between myself and my beliefs. And now my beliefs are winning out.

Let me explain how I see the battle. As a Hutterite child, I had little or no chance to grow up "free" as you and your brothers and sisters did. As soon as I had enough temper to raise a fist, the discipline began. Of course there was always plenty of love too—we are commanded to love and we are never alone. But to receive that love a child learns obedience. From kindergarten, where I played and learned to be quiet, to my years in the English and German schools, I learned not to decide for myself but to obey. I was very rarely strapped, though I think I was more disobedient in my mind than some of the others were. We were always punished immediately when we did wrong, and I never felt I was disciplined unfairly. After I was punished I was immediately accepted back into the group. I've always felt loved and cared for by my parents and everyone in our community.

I think that's one of the problems with "the world outside": there is no *group* to which I can belong. You've been a friend beyond what I could have expected, but your schooling is taking you more and more away from my type of life, and your marriage will mean that you've got to concentrate on life with Marlene and on building your career.

Career is another thing. If I had an engineering degree instead of home training in electrical repairs, I would be a valued person in Regina—look at the advertisements in the newspaper. I know you think I ought to enroll in technical school and get the certificate. And I agree that I've mastered about all this apprenticeship can teach. But the real problem is that no matter how far I progressed, I would be accepting a system I have learned to detest—the system of competition. If tomorrow I can get a little farther, make a little more money, climb over a few more people, I will be able to look down on them as they look down on me today. An apprentice is nothing, an engineer everything.

In the colony every job has importance. I knew when I cleaned out the cattle barns that my work meant as much to the community as the field manager's work did. I never felt envy for another person's importance—we were all doing a job together to survive.

You once accused us of being communists. But it's clear to me that totalitarian communism fails just where the Hutterites succeed. We have no poor, and we have no wealthy. Certainly this should be one of the goals of every Christian community. We truly have all things in common. More important than that, we understand God's rule over all parts of our lives. That rule is what makes obedience to our elders a more true freedom than I could find in the city. Here I have been alone. But I have found that being alone is too often lonely. I don't believe God created me to be lonely.

Once you called me a separatist, remember? I think I can answer that now because I see what we have separated from. Not from the good things of this world: we use modern machines, eat plenty of good food, enjoy wine and beer in moderation, build strong and warm houses. Nor have we separated from other churches (though they usually think so): most Hutterites will readily admit that many other people will share eternity with them.

But we *have* separated from war and violence. We have separated from a society that murders its living children before they are born, that strikes for higher wages but doesn't insist on delivering an honest day's work, that will sacrifice the wilderness to make profit on oil, that praises the equality of the sexes but suggests through every magazine and movie that females can be used simply as objects of sexual desire. I'm convinced it is right that I should be separate from all of this. What Christian shouldn't?

You'll notice I've left my stereo, my records, and the portable TV behind. They're yours; I'm embarrassed as I write this to remember how important it seemed to me that I should own those things for myself. I wish now I could get the lyrics of some of those songs out of my head.

Thinking about all of this, and much more, has led me to decide two things. With God's help, I want to be baptized, and I want to marry a Hutterite girl.

If I tried to bring in converts, I'd be excommunicated from the church. My job is to keep watch over my own flock—not to gather stray sheep. Converts to our way are very rare. You are born *a Hutterite.*

Hutterite preacher.
William Albert Allard,
"The Hutterites, Plain People of the West,"
National Geographic, July 1970

But why don't you just live our way? Maybe after you are here awhile, you will see that this is the only way to live.

Eli Walter, Hutterite.
William Albert Allard,
"The Hutterites, Plain People of the West,"
National Geographic, July 1970, pp. 102–3

Later that night a bunch of us sat in a dimly lighted bedroom, sipping cans of cold beer and singing songs about Montana cowboys. One of the women drew a harmonica from her apron pocket and played "Red River Valley." A 14-year-old girl brought out a guitar she wasn't supposed to have, and...softly sang a country-western song about young love. The boys teased the girls, and the men laughed at their own jokes, while wide-eyed children fell asleep, one by one, slumped in the arms of their parents.

There were many nights like that. Nights following days of hard work. Nights ending with a song, some gentle laughter, and a prayer of thanks.

To some, perhaps not very exciting. To the Hutterites, it is all they ask.

William Albert Allard, "The Hutterites, Plain People of the West," *National Geographic*, July 1970, pp. 102–3

Your parents had you baptized when you were a baby. That may have showed their confidence that God loved you, but how could it show your love for God? For me, baptism must be of far greater significance; it means *I* am willing to give myself totally to God's will for me. It's taken these years in the city and almost twenty years before that for me to know beyond doubt that I am willing to do that. Now that I have made up my mind, I'm ready to go back and receive instruction.

Will they receive me? Of course they will. The colony has shunned me ever since I left, but now that I've made my decision, they'll welcome me back. How do I know that? Partly because I've seen others return, but mainly because I know that once I admit my errors and submit again to the colony, they *must* receive me back. If that were not so, there would be no meaning to forgiveness, would there?

And then we'll begin the marriage plans for me—that's why I can say I'm not envying you! Sarah has not written once, but I've heard in roundabout ways that she expects me to return.

After the details have been worked out and her parents and colony have agreed, she will leave her colony and join mine. And I will be the head of my home. Don't tease me about that. I'll admit I intend to give Sarah more freedom than most of our wives have. You and Marlene can claim credit for that. But I also know she will want her life to "fit" with the colony's.

So we will raise a large family, and after some years—by the time you are president of a corporation—Sarah and I may be involved in beginning a new branch colony. Our colony had more than one hundred thirty persons before I left and the men were discussing possible moves almost every evening.

Does that sound dull? Not to me. The modern world I've seen convinced me that it has failed to show people how to live close to their God and their brothers and sisters in Christ. That's what we Hutterites have been trying to do for a long time. I think we've done a better job of it than anyone else, and that's why I'm going back to it.

Thanks for being a good friend. I'll think of you often. I hope you and Marlene will be happy and that you'll remember the stimulating talks and good times we had together. God bless you.

Your friend,
Jacob

FOR FURTHER READING

Allard, William Albert. "The Hutterites, Plain People of the West," *National Geographic,* July 1970.

An excellent, illustrated article (30 pages) on the Hutterites in the United States. Based on the author's personal contacts.

Bennett, John W. *Hutterite Brethren.* Stanford, Calif.: Stanford University Press, 1967.

Along with the next reference, provides in-depth studies of the Hutterites.

Hostetler, John. *Hutterite Society.* Baltimore: John Hopkins University Press, 1974.

Rideman, Peter. *Confession of Faith.* 2d Eng. ed. Rifton, N.Y.: The Plough Publishing House, 1970.

Originally published in 1545 and still the Hutterite confession of faith.
confession of faith.

Hutterite Children, Montana

SESSION GUIDE

CHALLENGE 7 HUTTERITES

A. Personal notes/questions on Challenge 7

B. Understanding the challenge

   1. Why did Jacob return to the Hutterite community?

   2. Do you sympathize at all with his feelings? Explain.

C. Our response

   1. Hutterites believe Acts 2:44–45 commands Christians to have all things in common. We disagree. Why? Does this passage say *anything* to us today?

2. In his *Confession of Faith* Peter Rideman clearly instructs his followers to withdraw from the world, citing such passages as 2 Corinthians 6:14–17 and John 15:18–19. Again, most Christians disagree with Rideman's interpretation. Why? How *are* Christians supposed to relate to the world? (See Matt. 28:19–20, 1 John 2:15, Rom. 12:1–2.)

3. If you were Thomas would you
   a. write Jacob a letter telling him you agree 100 percent with his decision, that he did the right thing, that you agree with the way he reads his Bible?

   b. write Jacob a letter explaining that while you as a Christian reject his view of the world, you think he did what was best for himself in returning to the Hutterite community and you will always regard him as a brother in Christ?

   c. write Jacob a letter of protest, pointing out that his biblical view of the world is incorrect and urging him to return to the city?

   d. other?

4. Compare your ideas with Response 7.

5. What can we learn from our Hutterite brothers and sisters in the Lord?

Peyote Meeting

NATIVE AMERICAN CHURCH

Founding: Although the drug peyote (pay-O-tee) was used among the Aztecs around 1560, the peyote cult (or Native American Church) was not formed until 1918 in Oklahoma. Its articles of incorporation said it was formed "to foster...religious believers in Almighty God and in the customs of the several tribes of Indians...in the worship of a heavenly Father and to promote morality, sobriety, industry, charity, and right living...and cultivate a spirit of self-respect and brotherly love and union among the members of the several tribes of Indians throughout the United States...with and through the sacramental use of peyote" (Edward Anderson, *Peyote: The Divine Cactus,* p. 39).

Following: Peyote (or the Native American Church) is the most widespread contemporary religion among Native Americans and Native Canadians, claiming a membership of about 250,000. The organization of the NAC is rather loose: large numbers of small, local groups are governed by councils or associations.

Faith: Many Indians call peyote an Indian form of Christianity, but there is much disagreement about the amount of Christianity found in the NAC. Some peyote cults are more Christianized than others. Common beliefs and practices include the following:
  *Peyote, a mind-expanding drug, obtained from the round top or button of the peyote cactus, is used sacramentally by the NAC

as a means of communicating with God. God has placed part of the Holy Spirit in the peyote, granting its use only to Indians (though whites are sometimes invited to participate in the ceremonies). Peyote is eaten as part of an all-night ceremony in a tepee or hogan. These ceremonies include prayer, singing, Bible reading (sometimes), eating peyote, and contemplation. During this time, the peyote "speaks" to the participant, imparting truth through visions promising forgiveness of sins and healing of the body. The worshiper believes he or she is in direct communication with God or Christ.

*Peyote is thought to have great healing powers. Special ceremonies are sometimes held for the sick.

*The peyote ethic includes belief in the Ten Commandments and the golden rule, in universal brotherhood of the Indian tribes, in care of the family, in self-reliance, and in avoidance of alcohol.

*There is one God (heavenly Father) who rules over all and is the source of all power. God is equated with the Great Spirit.

*Jesus is sometimes viewed as a rejected man caring for the rejected Indian, sometimes as a traditional hero, sometimes as a divine intercessor between God and humanity. The role of Christ is often vague; tribes differ in their beliefs about him. To many, Jesus and peyote are equally important representatives of God.

*God sent the Holy Spirit (Comforter) to the white race long ago; but the Spirit comes to the Indian in the form of peyote. In many tribes peyote is called the Peyote Spirit.

*The kingdom of God will be fulfilled when all Indian tribes have eaten the peyote. Then the world will be made over, believers will live on, and everything will be as God intended it.

*Traditional Indian beliefs (in such ancient mythical creatures as the Thunder Bird, the Mother of Mankind, the Moon, the Sun, the Fire) are at least as important as Christian beliefs.

*The Bible is referred to frequently among the more Christianized peyote cults, though it is often radically interpreted to conform to peyote beliefs.

At first I resisted Herbert Pritchard's suggestion that I attend a peyote meeting. But as I worked on my cycle that morning, I changed my mind. After all, I probably wouldn't get another chance, and I knew I had really hurt my friend when I attacked him for joining the Native American Church.

Herbert was my first-semester dorm mate—until he left school three months into the semester. His mission-school education, he explained, had misled him into thinking he would feel accepted at a Christian college. But the number of parties, and the drinks and drugs available at a few of them, had dismayed him; he had begun hiding out in the library, reading all he could find on Indian history. "Which isn't much," he told me. "Four books on my tribe. And the more I read, the angrier I get." He usually declined to say why.

Once, when I made a teasing remark about all the uranium money the tribe must have, he surprised me with an angry description of how the white government systematically destroyed the Navajo economy and replaced it with nothing—the money from the uranium, he said, would never amount to more than a few hundred dollars per person per year. What impressed me was not so much the argument as the fervor: in those few months Herbert seemed to be making really negative assessments of the white American culture he had chosen by enrolling at my school.

Now it was summer, and I was tuning my cycle in Herbert's backyard in Gallup. Herbert had just returned from downtown where he had been "making arrangements" for me to attend a peyote meeting. I wondered whether everything would be "arranged" to allay my suspicions. I had told Herbert what some of the missionaries had said about the addictive power of peyote and the drunken orgies at peyote meetings. He had laughed, but I could tell he was slightly angry.

"Sure," he said, "I know exactly what the missionaries think: if it's white, it's right. The peyote way is Indian so it must be wrong. Truth is, they don't know what they're talking about. Peyote won't hurt you. It may make you want to vomit, but you won't be sorry.

Brother we are told that you have been preaching to white people in this place; these people are our neighbors, we are acquainted with them. We will wait a little while, and see what effect your preaching has upon them. If we find it does them good, makes them honest and less disposed to cheat Indians, we will then consider again what you have said.

Seneca Chief Red Jacket to a missionary, 1805.
Carl F. Starkloff, *The People of the Center*, p. 122

Peyote is the Indians' Christ. You white people needed a man to show you the way, but the Indians have always been friends with the plants and have understood them. So to us the peyote came. And not to the whites.

Edward Anderson, *Peyote: The Divine Cactus*, p. 52

The Indians' means of achieving knowledge is superior to that of the white man. The latter learns from books what other people have to say; the former learns from peyote by direct experience. A Comanche once said, "The white man talks about Jesus; we talk to Jesus."

J. S. Slotkin, *The Peyote Religion*, pp. 99–100

Indians hold their services at night, while the white man sleeps, because God has time then for his Indian friends.

Humphrey Osmond, "Peyote Night"
(from Bernard Aaronson, *Psychedelics*, p. 75)

You will vomit your sins and be purified. To me, peyote is the voice of Jesus. It's God's way for the Navajo. The missionaries and traditionalists and Christians are all against it. But they won't seriously try it. They're afraid they'll learn how wrong they are. Have you ever smoked pot?"

"No. But I once had a roommate who did."

Herbert made a little hand gesture. "Then you know many of the claims about marijuana are false. It's not nearly as dangerous as they say it is. And peyote is even safer: it's not harmful to your body, and when its use is directed, it becomes a spiritual experience. Since it can't hurt you, why not try it?"

He explained that his brother was a road man and would be holding a meeting in Window Rock about fifteen miles northwest. All we had to do was get the cycle ready, put on clean clothes, and go.

Later that night when we arrived at the hogan, participants were already seated in a circle against the walls. Herbert showed me where to sit. He talked to the road man who sat behind a sort of earthen altar shaped like a moon. Then he returned and told me I was welcome but was not expected to pray or sing unless I wanted to. He whispered, "They don't want visitors who come just out of curiosity. I told them you were serious about this."

"I think I am serious," I said. "I'm a Christian who wants to know why you left the church."

The ceremony began as the road man took out the special peyote button and put it on the altar. I knew the service would have four parts, each beginning with participants smoking a cigarette and singing songs. Herbert had told me that much. As we lit our first cigarettes, he told me more. "Get rid of the bad thoughts while you smoke," he whispered. "There are many spirits coming and going. The road man has prayed that you will understand as much of this as you can."

Just the opposite was true. The water drum, the rattles, the feathers—I had no idea what they meant. When someone handed the peyote to me, I looked at Herbert for instructions. He showed me how to scrape a bit of the fuzzy part of the button. Then I chewed it down. It was like a hard, bitter nut. "Take two buttons," Herbert said. "You can take more later."

By then everyone around me was drumming and singing. One person drummed and the person next to him sang. My head was beginning to ache. My back and legs hurt from sitting too long on the floor. The bitter taste of the buttons lingered on my tongue, and the same sourness filled my stomach. I was afraid I would be sick.

In roughly twenty minutes things began to change. The hogan no longer seemed small and cramped; instead it felt spacious—big enough for many more than the fourteen or fifteen people present. The singing and drumming seemed softer and quieter than before; it had more melody. I could understand the praying now too, and I started feeling very sad. Herbert was still sitting next to me; he was singing and the man to his right was drumming. I wondered if I was supposed to be drumming for him too. I felt I should, but I knew I couldn't—I don't know how to drum at all. I felt I had let him down, but I was sure he wasn't angry at me.

I ate some more peyote buttons before they brought the midnight water in. And for the rest of the meeting the nausea disappeared. I experienced a change in perception, though perhaps I didn't think that then. The room was continually expanding, I felt no discomfort in my legs or back, and a warm feeling replaced the sadness.

Gradually the meaning of the songs and prayers changed too. At least I thought they changed because I was increasingly aware that no one was angry with me. I was talking or praying myself, telling the chief peyote that I was white and admitting I couldn't understand the Indian, that I wanted to be understood even though I couldn't understand.

While I was talking, I was aware in another part of my mind that probably only Herbert could hear me. And Herbert was still singing his own song.

After I finished my talk or prayer to chief peyote, I was very quiet for a long time. I knew I could stay there forever if I wanted to. I also knew that I wouldn't do that. Instead I would finish my cycle trip and try another semester of school in the fall.

Peyotism contains in its beliefs and values: elements of magical aid . . . , compensations for loss of status, a code of morality opposing drunkenness, adultery, and shiftlessness (the three plagues of reservation life), and hundreds of items designed to restore the self-respect of the Indian as an Indian.

Sylvia Thrupp, *Millennial Dreams in Action,* p. 212

Dear Heavenly Father,
We are representing our folks
under this teepee.
Dear Heavenly Father,
Dear Heavenly Father,
Bless these men that are
observers here.

Dear Heavenly Father,
These poor people surrendered
all their lands
To the Government of
Canada—their conditions
Are pitiful.
Dear Heavenly Father—bless my
people back home.

Prayer chanted in English at peyote ceremony. Humphrey Osmond, "Peyote Night" (from Bernard Aaronson, *Psychedelics,* pp. 72–3)

Their conditions are wretched. They are demoralized. Many of them hate and despise farming. The Native American Church is something of their own, born of their own misfortunes and developed from their pre-Columbian traditions. It has grown and flourished in spite of white men and this makes it even more precious to the Indian.

From a lecture by J. S. Slotkin.
Humphrey Osmond, "Peyote Night"
(from Bernard Aaronson, *Psychedelics,* p. 68)

After awhile I saw a set of lights. The center line of white light was so bright it seemed to pierce the walls of the hogan. Parallel to it were similar lines—bright lights of blue and red. Beams from the two colored lines shimmered and moved toward the central line.

For a long time I sat and watched. Though I'd never seen anything like this before, I was completely relaxed. I knew what the lines were. The white line was a road of knowledge—alone, by itself, with no one on it. On each side were people from different backgrounds, traveling parallel to the line of light—often reaching out, touching it, and drawing back. I tried to look as far as I could into the wall or the sky, following the lines to see where they met. But they did not meet. I am creating this out of my mind, I said, so I will *make* the lines meet. But they did not meet. I understood then that the ways whites and Indians take to knowledge were ways that did not meet. But this did not make me sad: I felt accepted by those who still sang and drummed around me.

When it was almost morning, the road man prayed over the morning water that the dawn woman brought. After that people took turns thanking chief peyote and the road man for the meeting and what it had done for them. I asked Herbert to thank them all. I did not know what the others had learned that night, or whether they felt cleansed, but that's the way I felt.

A morning breakfast had been prepared, but I suggested to Herbert we get back to Gallup so that I could make Albuquerque with time to spare.

The wind was cold as we came into Gallup so Herbert made coffee for me at his house. I didn't feel tired at all.

"What will you say about peyote?" Herbert asked.

"I honestly don't know. I think I learned a lot, but I can't put it into words yet."

"You believe Jesus is the truth and way and life. When peyote tells you the truth, isn't that Jesus or his Spirit talking?"

I couldn't answer: I didn't know enough. When I get back home, I've got to think this through and write him a long and careful letter.

FOR FURTHER READING

Aaronson, Bernard and Osmond, Humphrey, eds. *Psychedelics*. Cambridge, Mass.: Schenkman, 1971.

Contains an account by Humphrey Osmond entitled "Peyote Night" in which Mr. Osmond vividly describes his participation in a peyote ceremony.

Anderson, Edward. *Peyote: The Divine Cactus*. Tucson: University of Arizona Press, 1980.

La Barre, Weston. *The Peyote Cult*. Hamden, Conn.: Shoestring Press, 1964.

Lanternari, Vittorio. *The Religions of the Oppressed; A Study of Modern Messianic Cults*. New York: Knopf, 1963.

See chapter 2, "The Peyote Cult."

Slotkin, J. S. *The Peyote Religion*. New York: Octagon Books, 1975.

In a classic study, a scholar and former official of the NAC takes an extended look at the peyote cult.

Arrangement of a Navaho Peyote Meeting

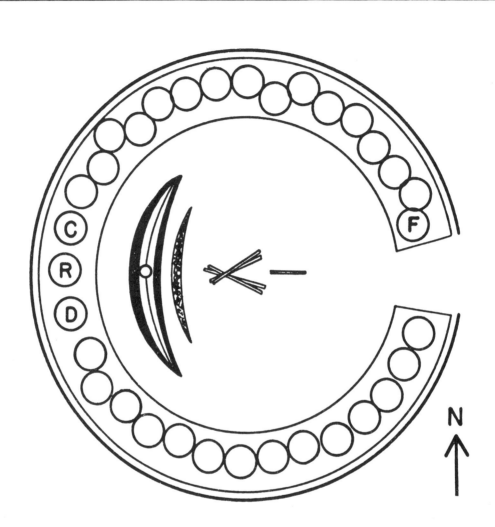

Arrangement of a Navaho peyote meeting. Outer circle represents hogan or tepee. Small circles represent participants (not segregated by sex). Lines inside outer circle represent area spread with blankets on which participants sit. *R* is road man, *D* is drummer man, *C* is cedar man, *F* is fire man. West to east in center appear: crescent moon earth "altar" with "peyote road" line down center and "chief peyote" on top; ash crescent; fire; "poker"; entrance. Not shown: road man's kit, drum, water bucket, dishes for peyote breakfast, woodpile.

The Peyote Religion Among the Navaho, p. 129

SESSION GUIDE

CHALLENGE 8   NATIVE AMERICAN CHURCH

A. Personal notes/comments on Challenge 8

B. Discussion questions (please read Response 8 before answering)

1. How important is the use of the drug peyote to the Native American Church? Was Herbert's friend, Dave, in any way helped by the peyote?

2. Are mind-expanding drugs such as peyote a legitimate aid to worship, to receiving truth (revelation) from God? Explain.

3. Why can't Herbert find what he's after in the traditional Christian church? What attracts him to peyote and the Native American Church?

4. Dave criticizes the Native American Church because it claims to speak to the Indian only (Response 8). Do you agree with the criticism? What Scriptures (in addition to Acts 15) or creeds address this issue? Would Herbert be justified in saying your church is restricted primarily to one race or nationality?

C. Summary

  1. All things considered, do you agree with Response 8's conclusion that the Native American Church is a cult that follows peyote, not Christ?

  2. Of the five apologetic methods (see back of textbook), which seems to be a good choice to use with members of the Native American Church?

  3. Have you learned anything helpful to your own Christianity from this brief look at the Native American Church? Please comment.

Bibliography

Aaronson, Bernard and Osmond, Humphrey, eds. *Psychedelics.* Cambridge, Mass.: Schenkman, 1971.

Allard, William Albert. "The Hutterites, Plain People of the West." *National Geographic,* July 1970.

Allen, Diogenes. *The Reasonableness of Faith.* Washington: Corpus Books, 1968.

Anderson, Edward. *Peyote: The Divine Cactus.* Tucson: University of Arizona Press, 1980.

Babbitt, Marcy. *Living Christian Science.* Englewood Cliffs, N.J.: Prentice-Hall, 1975.

Bennett, Wallace F. *Why I Am a Mormon.* New York: Thomas Nelson Inc., 1958.

Bjornstad, James. "The Pseudo Scholarship of Victor Paul Wierwille." *Contemporary Christianity,* vol. VIII, no. 2, January–February 1979.

Boa, Kenneth. *Cults, World Religions, and You.* Wheaton, Ill.: Victor Books, 1977.

Bradford, Charles E. *Preaching to the Times.* Washington: Review and Herald Pub. Assoc., 1975.

Brown, Ruth and Rosley, Joan. "Cult Rumors Follow Ministry to Tempe." *Tempe* (Ariz.) *Daily News,* 7 February 1981.

Clemens, Clara. *Awake to a Perfect Day.* New York: Citadel Press, 1956.

Dickinson, Eleanor and Benziger, Barbara. *Revival!* New York: Harper & Row, 1974.

Eddy, Mary Baker. *Manual of the Mother Church.* Boston: Published by the Trustees under the will of Mary Baker Eddy, 1936.
——————. *Science and Health with Key to the Scriptures.* Boston: Published by the Trustees under the will of Mary Baker Eddy, 1922.

Enroth, Ronald M. *Youth, Brainwashing, and the Extremist Cults.* Grand Rapids, Mich.: Zondervan Publishing House, 1977.

Facts about Christian Science. Boston: Christian Science Publishing Society, 1959.

Gottschalk, Stephen. *The Emergence of Christian Science in American Religious Life.* Berkeley: University of California Press, 1974.

Gruss, Edmond C. *Cults and the Occult in the Age of Aquarius.* Nutley, N.J.: Presbyterian and Reformed Pub. Co., 1974.

Hoekema, Anthony A. *The Four Major Cults.* Grand Rapids, Mich.: Wm. B. Eerdmans Pub. Co., 1963.

Jehovah's Witnesses in the 20th Century. New York: Watchtower Bible and Tract Society, Inc., 1979.

Kane, Steven M. "Holy Ghost People: The Snake-Handlers of Southern Appalachia." *Appalachian Journal,* vol. 1, Spring 1974, pp. 255–62.

Kirban, Salem. *Jehovah's Witnesses.* Huntingdon Valley, Pa.: S. Kirban Inc., 1972.

Kuyvenhoven, Andrew. "It's Time to Burn the Wooden Shoes." *The Banner,* 3 November 1980, pp. 7–8.

Leishman, Thomas L. *Why I Am a Christian Scientist.* New York: Thomas Nelson Inc., 1958.

Martin, Walter R. *The Maze of Mormonism.* Grand Rapids, Mich.: Zondervan Publishing House, 1962.

"Mormonism Enters New Era." *Time,* 7 August 1978.

Mouw, Richard. "CRC—A Multiracial Community." *The Banner,* 3 November 1980, p. 9.

Nichol, Francis D. *Answers to Objections.* Washington, D.C.: Review and Herald Pub. Assoc., 1952.

Paxton, Geoffrey J. *The Shaking of Adventism.* Grand Rapids, Mich.: Baker Book House, 1978.

Pelton, Robert W. and Carden, Karen W. *Snake Handlers: God-fearers? Or Fanatics?* Nashville: Thomas Nelson Inc., 1974.

Plantinga, Cornelius, Jr. *Beyond Doubt.* Grand Rapids, Mich.: Board of Publications of the Christian Reformed Church, 1980.

Richardson, Don. *The Peace Child.* Glendale, Calif.: G/L Regal Books, 1974.

Ridemann, Peter. *Confession of Faith.* 2d Eng. ed. Rifton, N.Y.: Plough Publishing House, 1970.

Rosten, Leo. *Religions of America.* New York: Simon and Schuster, 1975.

Slotkin, James S. *The Peyote Religion.* New York: Octagon Books, 1975.

Smith, Joseph. *Book of Mormon.* Salt Lake City, Utah: The Church of Jesus Christ of Latter-day Saints, 1957.

——————. *Doctrine and Covenants.* Salt Lake City, Utah: The Church of Jesus Christ of Latter-day Saints, 1957.

——————. *The Pearl of Great Price.* Salt Lake City, Utah: The Church of Jesus Christ of Latter-day Saints, 1957.

Snook, John B. *Going Further.* Englewood Cliffs, N.J.: Prentice-Hall, 1973.

Sparks, Jack. *The Mindbenders.* Nashville: Thomas Nelson Inc., 1977.

Starkes, M. Thomas. *Confronting Popular Cults.* Nashville: Broadman Press, 1972.

Starkloff, Carl F. *The People of the Center.* New York: Seabury Press, 1974.

Swan, Jon. "The 400-Year-Old Commune." *Atlantic,* November 1972, pp. 90–100.

Thrupp, Sylvia L. *Millennial Dreams in Action.* The Hague: Mouton, 1962.

The Truth Shall Make You Free. New York: Watchtower Bible and Tract Society, Inc., International Bible Students Assoc., 1943.

Van Dam, C. and Van Doren, G. *Test the Spirits.* Winnipeg: Premier Publishing, 1973.

The Watchtower 75–681. New York: Watchtower Bible and Tract Society, Inc., 15 November 1954.

White, Ellen Gould. *Testimonies for the Church,* vols. 1–9. Oakland, Calif.: Pacific Press, 1882–1909.

Wierwille, Victor Paul. *Jesus Christ Is NOT God.* New Knoxville, Ohio: American Christian Press, 1975.

——————. *Power for Abundant Living,* New Knoxville, Ohio: American Christian Press, 1971.

FIVE APOLOGETIC APPROACHES

The chart below outlines five basic ways to defend your faith. Remember that in actual practice, emphasizing the love of God and witnessing with your life are at least as important as using any of these approaches. But knowing about the approaches will give you a starting point, a way to organize your own thinking and a plan to present your faith to others.

Your Reasons teacher will give you additional information on any of these approaches.

	ADVANTAGES	DISADVANTAGES
COMMON GROUND Begins with a friendly discussion of what the two faiths have in common. Then attempts to show that what the other faith believes is only partially true and that the Christian faith provides a deeper, more complete truth, a better perspective on the world, a better answer to the questions and problems.	Keeps the discussion conversational, low-key, reasonable.	Can be seen by opponent as compromising; may make your faith seem weak to other person.
CONFRONTATION Directly attacks (confronts) the contrasting faith, trying to show that its beliefs are either unrealistic or logically inconsistent and that, if pushed to their logical conclusions, these beliefs will be untenable and/or unlivable. Finally, may present the Christian system as the only one that is realistic and consistent.	Other person knows clearly where you stand. No waffling. Also appeals to those who value logic, consistency.	May antagonize the other person, not convince him, especially if he is so committed to his faith that he won't even discuss its flaws.

NEED-NOURISHMENT

Begins by probing what deep, inner needs are met by the contrasting faith, needs such as the desire for security, for self-esteem, for belonging, for understanding and beauty. Then shows that Christianity and Christ provide more than enough nourishment to live meaningfully, more than any other faith or belief system.

Addresses the life experiences of a person. Appeals to deep psychological and spiritual needs.

May not be effective with those whose needs were not met in the past by the Christian church, and whose needs are apparently now fully satisfied within the cult or sect.

OFFENSE

Begins by trying to remove unnecessary offenses (objections, obstacles) the contrasting faith raises against Christianity. Accomplished by correcting misunderstandings or misrepresentations of Christianity. Finally attempts to bring out the *real* differences between Christianity and the contrasting faith, making what is the necessary and unavoidable offense unmistakably clear.

Helpful when a person obviously has wrong notions about Christianity. Helpful for exposing real, important differences.

Could be ineffective if the other person's wrong notions about Christianity are based on her personal experience with the church and Christians.

TEST OF TRADITION

Simply shows that those who hold other positions have departed from the original orthodox/Christian faith. They have failed the test of tradition and have betrayed the authority they pretend to recognize (the Bible or the church or Christ).

Especially helpful for sects with Christian roots. Encourages genuine discussion of authorities (Bible, church, Christ) held in common.

Sects and cults often adhere rigidly to their interpretation of Scripture. Also, requires thorough knowledge of Scripture and traditional orthodox beliefs.

**Responses
to the
challenges
are to be
kept in the
attached
envelope.** ➡